Facing Death and

and

Eternity

with

Confidence

Questions and Answers Concerning Death

DOUG KNOX

ISBN 978-1-64458-673-0 (paperback)
ISBN 978-1-64458-674-7 (digital)

Christian Faith Publishing, Inc.
832 Park Avenue
Meadville, PA 16335
www.christianfaithpublishing.com

Printed in the United States of America

Contents

Introduction

There is no comfortable way to begin a conversation on the subject before us today. No matter how real, how personal, or to what degree we have experienced this subject, it is never an easy one to deal with. In almost every case, it is the last thing anyone wants to talk about.

However, in reality, it should be the first and most important subject because thus far, only two people from the beginning of time have ever escaped its effects.

The subject I'm talking about is death. All of us know that someday the grim reaper will come to harvest our soul, and our life on earth will cease to be. Will this be the end? Will we cease to exist? Is there an afterlife? If there is, where will it be and to what can it be compared?

The questions are numerous and the answers are few, that is, credible answers that will give a measure of hope and peace to the individual who is facing death or one who is mourning the departure of a loved one. I suppose unexpected and sudden deaths are probably the hardest not only to accept but to find comfort from because of the question why. Why did this happen and why now? It could not have happened at a worse time even, though there is never a good time for death to come.

Even when death is expected because of some incurable sickness, we are never honestly ready for that day to come. Naturally, we desire to hang on to them for as long as possible. Even when their suffering seems to be more than they can bear and we want relief for them, death is the last thing we desire for them.

Nevertheless, the inevitable happens. Now we are faced with grief, loneliness, despair, and a thousand unanswered questions. They will be missed, and we will wonder how we will make it without them. If only we could know what happens to them, where they are, and what they are doing, then the loss might be a little easier to bear.

Is there any reliable source that can bring hope and peace? Yes. That source is the Word of God—the Bible. Everybody has an opinion, but the Lord Jesus Christ has the answers. He and He alone knows all about death. He knows its origin, the sorrows acquainted with it, the separation involved, and He understands the why of it. For in the day of His death, He said, "*My God, my God, why hast thou forsaken me?*" (Mark 15:34, KJV).

It is said of Him, "*He is… a man of sorrows, and acquainted with grief*" (Isaiah 53:3). If there is anyone who understands the depths of our sorrows and grief, it is the Lord Jesus Christ.

The shortest verse in the English translation of the Bible speaks volumes. At the grave of Lazarus, in John 11:35, these two words appear: "*Jesus wept.*" Who would ever think, hope, or imagine that a god—any god—would even acknowledge much less shed a tear for his lowly creation. Yet Jesus, God in human flesh, not only notices the lone sparrow that falls to the ground, but He wept at the graveside of a beloved friend. He is truly touched with the feelings of our infirmities. He knows the depth of our sorrows; He sympathizes with our grief and is able to provide mercy and grace in the midst of it all.

How is He capable of entering into our sorrows and grief? How is He able to understand our fears? It's because He has experienced the sting of death. No one can fully understand and sympathize with another unless they have personally walked a mile in their shoes. However, He walked more than a mile; He finished the journey. And having experienced death, He fully understands the fears we face.

Hebrews 2:9 says, "*But we see Jesus, who was made a little lower than the angels for the suffering of death, crowned with glory and honour; that he by the grace of God should taste death for every man.*"

Hebrews 5:7 reads, "*Who in the days of his flesh, when he had offered up prayers and supplications with strong crying and tears unto him that was able to save him from death, and was heard in that he feared.*"

Yes, there are times when all human affection and comfort fails in the midst of our grief. Times when we not only feel alone but even desire to be left alone. It is in times of solitude that those who know the Lord Jesus Christ as their personal Saviour can find comfort and peace, which passes all understanding. How? Knowing the knife of grief, sorrow, crying, and fear first pierced His heart before it did ours. Jesus has experienced firsthand the death of a loved one and His own death. Personal experience qualifies Him to be the "Captain of our Salvation" (Hebrews 2:10). With an experienced Captain at the helm, we can face death and eternity confidently knowing He has sailed the charted course before us and is sufficiently equipped to sustain us when it comes to our turn to sail these troubled waters.

He is not "the bridge over troubled waters" but the "Captain" of your vessel in the midst of troubled waters. He's the Friend when no friends can be found. He dries the tears when they flow like a river. He's by your side when times get rough, when the night falls, the darkness engulfs you and pain is your companion. He will comfort you, never leave you, and will guarantee you will safely reach the other side.

Isaiah 43:2–3 reads, "*When thou passest through the waters, I will be with thee: and through the rivers, they shall not overflow thee: when thou walkest through the fire, thou shalt not be burned; neither shall the flame kindle upon thee. For I am the Lord thy God… thy Saviour.*"

Yes, death is not an easy subject to talk about. However, to the survivor, the comfort, peace, and confidence you desire depend upon the source of your information. Can you say with absolute confidence that your source is dependable and trustworthy? You can if your source is the Word of God, the Bible.

With that said, let's begin facing death and eternity with confidence.

Personal Experience

It is never easy to stand by the bedside of a loved one who is facing their final moments on this side of eternity. Such was the case on February 2, 2013.

It had been a long night. I had agreed to stay with my dad and would let the rest of the family know if any significant changes took place. The night passed rather quietly, and when some of the family entered the next morning, I headed home for a shower and a couple of winks of sleep.

Around ten in the morning, I proceeded to get up and get dressed to return to my dad's bedside. This time, it would not be the casual dress but a coat and tie. The reason being, I was my dad's pastor.

As soon as I entered the room, my sister-in-law said, "Official business this time," to which I nodded. Deep down, I knew this day was it. The time of my dad's departure had come, and it would be my duty and privilege to read a passage of scripture to him and have a word of prayer.

Though Dad was incapable of responding to anything read or prayed, I guess it was really for the family that had gathered in his presence. But what does one say at a time like this? What does one read or pray when hearts are broken and death is about to separate us one from the other?

Since my dad was a Christian, the passage I read was 2 Corinthians 5:1–8.

For we know that if our earthly house of this tabernacle were dissolved, we have a building of God, an house not made with hands, eternal in the heavens.

For in this we groan, earnestly desiring to be clothed upon with our house which is from heaven:

If so be that being clothed we shall not be found naked.

For we that are in this tabernacle do groan, being burdened: not for that we would be unclothed, but clothed upon, that mortality might be swallowed up of life.

Now he that hath wrought us for the selfsame thing is God, who also hath given unto us the earnest of the Spirit.

Therefore we are always confident, knowing that, whilst we are at home in the body, we are absent from the Lord:

(For we walk by faith, not by sight:)

We are confident, I say, and willing rather to be absent from the body, and *to be present with the Lord.*

My dad, like many other Christians before him, was fixing to put off this body of clay and put on a new body which is not subject to sin, sickness, or death. When he drew his last breath on earth, he would take in his first celestial breath on the other side. This is the comfort and promise God has given to those who repent of their sin and trust Jesus Christ as their personal Saviour.

Were there tears? Of course. There's nothing wrong with weeping for a departing family member or friend. Remember, Jesus wept at the grave of His friend Lazarus (John 11:35). The Bible says in 1 Thessalonians 4:13, *"But I would not have you to be ignorant, brethren, concerning them which are asleep, that ye sorrow not, even as others which have no hope."*

For the Christian and their departed loved ones who are Christians, we are not to weep as "*others which have no hope.*" The reason being, we understand what transpires when a loved one dies.

According to the Word of God, Dad was trading in, so to speak, that old earthly and frail body for a new one "*not made with hands, but eternal in the heavens.*" We also knew when he drew his last breath here, he would be "*absent from the body*" and immediately "*present with the Lord.*" And finally, we knew this was not the end. We were not saying goodbye but see you later.

Both of my parents have gone home to be with the Lord. And the day is coming when I and my siblings will be reunited with them, never to be separated again. This is the hope every Christian has.

Death is an inescapable part of life. Every individual has an appointment with death. Hebrews 9:27 read, "*And as it is appointed unto men once to die, but after this the judgment.*" The question is, are you prepared when that time comes? See, preparation for death must be made while we are alive because after death, it will be too late. In the words of Amos, the prophet: "*Prepare to meet thy God,*" for all of us have an appointment with God (Amos 4:12). Are you ready for that day? If not, you can be.

The Origin of Death

Why do people die? Multitudes of answers could be given ranging from murder, disease, accidents, suicide, and the list goes on. However, death has not always existed. After God created all things, including humanity, there was an undetermined length of time in which nothing—nature, the animal kingdom, nor humanity—experienced death.

So what changed? The Book of Genesis reveals the answer. God the Creator created everything in six literal days. The highlight of His creation was man. In Genesis 1:26–27, 2:7, the Bible says, *"And God said, Let us make man, after our image, after our likeness... So God created man in his own image, in the image of God created he him; male and female created he them. And the Lord God formed man of the dust of the ground, and breathed into his nostrils the breath of life; and man became a living soul."*

Next, God planted a garden and placed the man there in order to take care of it. Then God gave Adam simple instructions, which would prove his loyalty and love to God. *"And the Lord God commanded the man, saying, Of every tree of the garden thou mayest eat freely: But of the tree of the knowledge of good and evil, thou shalt not eat of it: for in the day thou eatest thereof thou shalt surely die"* (Genesis 2:16–17).

From these two passages of scripture, three eternal truths are set forth. *One:* God has a will and He expresses it to mankind. *Second:* that man was created with a freewill, the ability to choose whether to obey or disobey God. *Third:* there are consequences for disobeying

God's command. These three things have existed and will continue as long as man is on earth.

When we enter chapter 3 of Genesis, we find the results of Adam's choice. "*And when the woman saw that the tree was good for food, and pleasant to the eyes, and a tree to be desired to make one wise, she took of the fruit thereof, and did eat, and gave also unto her husband with her; and he did eat. And the eyes of them both were opened, and they knew they were naked; and they sewed fig leaves together, and made themselves aprons. And they heard the voice of the LORD God walking in the garden in the cool of the day: and Adam and his wife hid themselves from the presence of the LORD God amongst the trees of the garden*" (Genesis 3:6–8).

Did Adam die? The answer is yes and no. How can that be true? Well, two facts need to be understood at this point. First, there are three types of death in the Bible. They are spiritual death (Ephesians 2:1), physical death (Hebrews 9:27), and the eternal or second death (Revelation 20:11–15). Second, neither of these deaths teach the cessation nor the annihilation of life. Death, from a biblical viewpoint, is simply a "separation." Here's a brief account of the three deaths:

Spiritual Death

"*And you hath he quickened, who were dead in trespasses and sin*" (Ephesians 2:1). When Adam disobeyed God by eating of the forbidden tree, he sinned against God. Here's a biblical definition of sin: "*Therefore to him that knoweth to do good, and doeth it not, to him it is sin*" (James 4:17). Adam knew what to do but chose to disobey God; therefore, he sinned.

Now the Bible says, "*Wherefore as by one man [Adam] sin entered into the world*" (Romans 5:12). Since we are all the descendants of Adam and have received his sinful nature, then we are all sinners. "*For all have sinned and come short of the glory of God*" (Romans 3:23). It is the sinful nature received from Adam that renders us dead spiritually before God—physically alive but spiritually dead or separated. The prophet Isaiah describes this perfectly: "*Behold, the Lord's hand is not shortened, that he cannot save; neither his ear heavy, that he can-*

not hear: But your iniquities have separated between you and your God, and your sins have hid his face from you, that he will not hear" (Isaiah 59:1–2). The day Adam sinned in the garden, he died spiritually in that he was separated from God as indicated by these words: "*Adam and his wife hid themselves from the presence of the LORD God amongst the trees of the garden.*"

Physical Death

"*And as it is appointed unto men once to die, but after this the judgment*" (Hebrews 9:27). From the scriptures, it is abundantly clear Adam did not physically die the very day he ate of the forbidden tree. As a matter of fact, when Adam and Eve ate the fruit of that tree, they had no children. Yet in chapters 3 and 5, we find that they had three sons: Cain, Abel, and Seth. Then we read: "*And all the days that Adam lived were nine hundred and thirty years: and he died*" (Genesis 5:5). This is physical death. Adam is now separated physically from his family. They would never be able to see or fellowship with Adam again as long as they lived. Why? Romans 5:12 says, "*Wherefore as by one man* (Adam) *sin entered into the world, and death* [physical] *by sin; and so death* [physical] *passed upon all men, for that all have sinned.*" Herein is the origin of death and the reason people die every day. Death started with Adam's disobedience to God, and because we are his descendants, we will face death too. "*For in Adam all die*" (1 Corinthians 15:22).

Adam died *spiritually* the day he ate of the forbidden tree. However, *physical death* did not occur until he was "*nine hundred and thirty years*" old.

Eternal or the Second Death

"*And death and hell were cast into the lake of fire. This is the second death. And whosoever was not found written in the book of life was cast into the lake of fire*" (Revelation 20:14–15). Without going into great detail, I'd like to briefly mention a couple of things about this.

First, this death is not an appointed death, like physical death. Let me try to explain. Because we are the descendants of Adam, we are all spiritually separated from God because we have all sinned. We have no choice in this matter at all. We are not sinners because we have sinned; we sin because we are sinners by the nature we inherited from Adam. Therefore, we all have an appointment with physical death. It is a mandatory appointment. We have no choice in the matter, and one day we will die physically.

Second, we do have a choice when it comes to the second death. The power of the second death over an individual is solely based on what he or she does with Jesus Christ. Every person has a choice as to whether or not they will receive or reject Jesus Christ as their personal Saviour. Those who receive Jesus Christ as their Saviour, their names are recorded in the Book of Life, and the second death will have no power over them. However, those who reject Him as their Saviour, they will be cast into the lake of fire which is the second death. Those individuals will be *eternally separated* from God and be tormented in the lake of fire forever.

The question that must be asked: What have you done with Jesus Christ, God's Son? Have you received or rejected Him? My friend, your eternal destiny is determined by your choice!

The Description of Death

How does one go about describing death? If asked to describe a sunset, a flower, a garden, the mountains, a bride, or little baby, well, the words would be endless. Death, on the other hand, is all bees without the honey.

Generally speaking, the only good comments said about death are after someone has had a long hard battle with some incurable disease. Those comments are usually, at least they are not *suffering anymore*, or they are in a *better place*. These are meant to bring some comfort to the survivors.

However, the Bible gives several descriptions of death. These of course are from God's viewpoint, not man's. I would like to share ten ways in which God views the death of a man.

Returning to the Dust

> *In the sweat of thy face shalt thou eat bread,* till thou return unto the ground; for out of it wast thou taken: for dust thou art, and unto dust shalt thou return... *All go to one place,* all are of the dust *and all turn to dust again... Then shall the dust return to the earth as it was and* the spirit shall return unto God who gave it.
> —Genesis 3:19; Ecclesiastes 3:20, 12:7

We have all heard the phrase "Ashes to ashes, dust to dust" at one time or another. In most cases, it is used in reference to the death and burial of an individual. Though the exact phrase isn't found in the Bible, the concept is biblical. The exact phrase comes from the Book of Common Prayer, and it is based on Genesis 3:19, 18:27; Job 30:19; and Ecclesiastes 3:20.

Often, a version of this prayer is heard at the gravesite. "*In sure and certain hope of the resurrection to eternal life through our Lord Jesus Christ, we commend to Almighty God our dearly beloved; and we commit his/ her body to the ground; earth to earth; ashes to ashes, dust to dust. The Lord bless him and keep him, the Lord make his face to shine upon him and be gracious unto him and give him peace. Amen.*"

In this prayer, we are reminded of several things. First, the frailty of humanity; "*earth to earth; ashes to ashes, dust to dust.*" Second, death is not the end of life: in "*sure and certain hope of the resurrection.*" Third, that eternal life as far as heaven is a concern, comes through Jesus alone: "*to eternal life through our Lord Jesus Christ.*" Fourth, (this applies to the saved alone), God will bless, keep, be gracious to, and will give them peace. Amen.

Evolution would have you to believe that man evolved from some lower form of life. Yet the Bible clearly states that God created man out of the dust of the ground and God breathed into his nostrils the breath of life and man became a living soul. "*And the LORD God formed man of the dust of the ground, and breathed into his nostrils the breath of life; and man became a living soul*" (Genesis 2:7).

If we were to read no further in the Bible, we would come to the conclusion that man is a dichotomy. That he is a material (body) and immaterial (soul) being. And in this category alone, material and immaterial, that would be true.

However, upon further investigation, the Bible reveals that we are a trichotomy. "*And the very God of peace sanctify you wholly; and I pray God your whole spirit, and soul, and body be preserved blameless unto the coming of our Lord Jesus Christ*" (1 Thessalonians 5:23). Of these three parts, only one is susceptible to death: the body. When the body dies, it returns to the ground or dust from where it came. However, the soul and spirit return to God Who gave it. Thus, it could be said that man is also temporal (body) and eternal (soul and spirit).

The Old and the New Testaments verify these truths: *"And many of them that sleep in the dust of the earth shall awake, some to everlasting life, and some to shame and everlasting contempt"* (Daniel 12:2). *"Therefore we are always confident, knowing that, whilst we are at home in the body, we are absent from the Lord: We are confident, I say, and willing rather to be absent from the body and present with the Lord"* (2 Corinthians 5:6, 8).

Nature proves the Bible to be true. If the body is left in its natural state after death, it would soon deteriorate and return to the dust from where it came. No one questions the *destination of the human body*; that's a given. However, the eternal destiny of the soul and spirit is a horse of a different color. Where will you spend eternity?

Being Dissolved

> *For we know that if our earthly house of this*
> *tabernacle were dissolved, we have a building*
> *of God, an house not made with hands,*
> *eternal in the heavens. For in this we groan,*
> *earnestly desiring to be clothed upon with*
> *our house which is from heaven: If so be that*
> *being clothed we shall not be found naked.*
> —2 Corinthians 5:1–8

This passage may seem a little strange to the casual reader. At first glance, one may think the writer is speaking of a brick-and-mortar-type house. However, he is not speaking of that kind of dwelling. He is exactly comparing our body to a house.

The following verses verify this. *"Therefore we are always confident, knowing that, whilst we are at home in the body, we are absent from the Lord: We are confident, I say, and willing rather to be absent from the body, and to be present with the Lord"* (2 Corinthians 5:6, 8).

This passage reinforces how frail and temporal the physical body really is. Note the descriptive word God uses for the body—*tabernacle*. It is a word that in the Greek language means booth or tent. If you have ever been camping, a tent is okay to live in for a few days. However, you would not want to make it a permanent dwelling.

To strengthen the argument that the body is temporal, God said, "*If our earthly house of this tabernacle were dissolved.*" The word *dissolve* doesn't mean to vanish as we might imagine. It comes from a Greek word which means to "loose or unloose what was before bound." It is a picture of loosening the burdens that animals would carry.

With age, the body begins to wear out. The aches become unbearable. Disease and illness infiltrate the body. The immune system is weak and unable to ward off the reoccurrence of one sickness after the other. Sometimes, it is so overwhelming. The individual reaches a breaking point, desiring to die rather than live. They are ready to be freed from the pain and suffering of this body. Death is that which unleashes them from the physical suffering they are bound with.

Thus, the saying, "At least they are not suffering anymore." Let's ponder that statement for a moment. It is true that such an individual has ceased from their physical agony. Nevertheless, one must remember that the body and the pain in that body are temporal. The body, at death, returns to the dust from where it came, but the soul and spirit are eternal.

When death occurs, we do not become disembodied spirits as some might think. Listen, "*Earnestly desiring to be clothed upon with our house which is from heaven: If so be that being clothed we shall not be found naked. For we that are in this tabernacle do groan, being burdened: not for that we would be unclothed, but clothed upon, that mortality might be swallowed up of life*" (2 Corinthians 5:2–4).

The "body" is designed by God (*we have a building of God*). It is suitable for our eternal abode. For the Christian, his or her body will be suited for heaven where there is no more pain, sorrow, and death. In like manner, the non-Christian will have a body designed to withstand the pain, agony, and torments of hell. Even though his or her suffering has ended on earth, it has just begun in hell and will last for eternity.

Therefore, the phrase "At least they are not suffering anymore" is only true if the deceased was a Christian. If not, their temporal suffering was traded in for eternal suffering.

Departing

> *For I am in a strait betwixt two, having*
> *a desire to depart and be with Christ;*
> *which is far better: Nevertheless to abide*
> *in the flesh is more needful for you.*
> —Philippians 1:23–24

There are many departures in life. Some are essential, such as leaving for work. While others are more enjoyable, such as vacation or retirement. However, there is a departure in which, like the apostle Paul, people struggle with. They are torn between the desires to be with the Lord, that is, to die or to stay here with their loved ones.

Doctors, nurses, home health caregivers, and countless others have witnessed multitudes on their deathbeds hanging on when there is no medical reason for them to be alive. They will sometimes ask the family if there is someone the patient has not seen or heard from. Then, without fail, when that person has come and spent some time with them, they quietly slip off into eternity.

Such was the case with an elderly widow who had no family left to say goodbye to. As a member of the church which I pastor, there was a couple in the church she loved dearly and who were on vacation. With the joint power of attorney shared with a friend of hers, there was a decision which needed to be made concerning her life, and we didn't want to make it without her dearest friends being involved.

Long story short, the couple returned from vacation and after learning of her condition came to the hospital to visit her. Now let me pause a moment to explain what the word *depart* in our verse means. It is a Greek word which has reference to pulling up the anchor of a ship and hoisting up the sails in order to leave port for a better destination.

Once this couple came and spent some time with her, as we stood just outside her door discussing our options, she pulled up anchor, hoisted up the sails, and quietly departed for a better destination.

The child of God is heading for a "better country," but not so for the unbeliever. Squire Parsons wrote a song about this place called Beulah Land. He talks about a country that he has never seen yet longs for, a country where there are no sad goodbyes and it is eternal. Yet that country lay on the other side of the river, and that river is symbolic of death.

Hebrews 11:16 reads, "*But now they desire a better country, that is, an heavenly: wherefore God is not ashamed to be called their God: for he hath prepare for them a city.*"

Death is the doorway that leads to this heavenly country, and for the child of God, it's not goodbye. It's pulling up anchor and setting sail homeward! As I said earlier, Jesus is not the bridge over troubled waters. He is the captain of the ship and we never sail alone. "*Yea, though I walk through the valley of the shadow of death, I will fear no evil: for thou art with me; thy rod and thy staff they comfort me*" (Psalm 23:4).

A Putting Off

> *Yea, I think it meet, as long as I am in this*
> *tabernacle, to stir you up by putting you*
> *in remembrance; Knowing that shortly I*
> *must put off this my tabernacle, even as*
> *our Lord Jesus Christ hath shewed me.*
> —2 Peter 1:13–14

What a description Peter gives concerning death. The tabernacle, which is the body, is said to be "put off," discarded as an old garment when it is worn out.

Some things get better with age. There is nothing like an old pair of shoes, a ragged pair of blue jeans, an old flannel shirt, and a faded-out denim jacket. They fit and feel like nothing else will. I have worn things like these to the embarrassment of my wife and have worn them until they were nothing but threads. Today, I have an old denim jacket I love to wear and my wife will be so glad when I get rid of it.

Nevertheless, this body doesn't get better with age. As an elderly gentleman told me one day, "Getting old ain't for sissies." The Apostle Paul tells us, "*For we that are* in this tabernacle do groan, *being burdened: not for that we would be unclothed, but clothed upon, that mortality might be swallowed up of life*" (2 Corinthians 5:4).

J.V. McGee said that his wife would tell him, "You shouldn't groan so much."

He would reply, "I'm just being scriptural."

Yes, this body will get old and wear out if we live long enough. There will be aches, pains, and even some parts that will quit working before we die.

Solomon describes how our bodies break down with age.

> *In the day when the keepers of the house shall tremble* [hands], *and the strong men shall bow themselves* [backs], *and the grinders cease because they are few* [teeth], *and those that look out of the windows be darkened* [eyes],*
>
> *And the doors shall be shut in the streets, when the sound of the grinding is low* [hearing], *and he shall rise up at the voice of the bird, and all the daughters of musick shall be brought low;*
>
> *Also when they shall be afraid of that which is high, and fears shall be in the way, and the almond tree shall flourish* [hair], *and the grasshopper shall be a burden, and desire shall fail* [impotent]: *because man goeth to his long home* [the grave], *and the mourners go about the streets:*

> *Or ever the silver cord be loosed, or the golden bowl be broken, or the pitcher be broken at the fountain, or the wheel broken at the cistern.*
>
> *Then shall the dust return to the earth as it was: and the spirit shall return unto God who gave it.* (Ecclesiastes 12:3–7)

Like a worn-out garment, this body will be laid aside for a new one. We will receive an eternal body. A body, like unto the resurrected body of Christ (Philippians 3:20–21).

Requiring the Soul

> *And I will say to my soul, Soul, thou hast much goods laid up for many years; take thine ease, eat, drink, and be merry. But God said unto him, Thou fool, this night thy soul shall be required of thee: then whose shall those things be, which thou hast provided. So is he that layeth up treasures for himself, and is not rich toward God.*
> —Luke 12:19–21

George MacDonald said, "You don't have a soul. You are soul."

Lehman Strauss said, "Man not only has a living soul but he is a living soul."

The "soul" is the immaterial and eternal part of man. It is not subject to death and is that which gives life and consciousness to each individual. Without the soul, the body is lifeless or dead.

In 1 Kings 17:17–22, we read where Elijah asked God to restore life to a little boy who had died. His prayer went like this: "*O LORD my God, hast thou brought evil upon the widow with whom I sojourn, by slaying her son... O Lord my God, I pray thee, let this child's soul come into him again. And the Lord heard the voice of Elijah; and the soul of the child came into him again, and he revived.*"

Also, in Genesis 35:18–19, "*And it came to pass, as her soul was in departing, (for she died) that she called his name Ben-oni… And Rachel died, and was buried in the way to Ephrath, which is Beth-lehem.*"

Our "soul" came from God (Genesis 2:7). The breath of God gave Adam's lifeless body life and consciousness, and man *became a living soul.* Our soul belongs to God. "*As I live, saith the Lord God… Behold, all souls are mine*" (Ezekiel 18:3–4). Therefore, we are responsible to, accountable to, and have an appointment with the "Judge of all the earth." Why?

The soul is the seat of our affections and determines the appetites of the body. It is the seat of our passions, feelings, and desires. The soul determines whether the body will be used as an instrument of righteousness or unrighteousness.

The soul of the rich man, in our text, reveals that he had no time or concern about God, just himself. Listen to his words: "*Soul, thou hast much goods laid up for many years; take thine ease, eat, drink, and be merry.*" He had made provisions for the present but failed to provide for eternity. Therefore, Jesus called him a fool.

Why? Well, there are two reasons why Jesus could have called this man a fool. First, this man could have been an atheist. "*The fool hath said in his heart, There is no God*" (Psalm 14:1). Second, he could be like many are today: he believed in God but lived as if he was not accountable to God. Listen: "*Then said Saul, I have sinned: return, my son David: for I will no more do thee harm, because my soul was precious in thine eyes this day: behold, I have played the fool, and have erred greatly*" (1 Samuel 26:21).

Saul is not proclaiming atheism by his statement "I have played the fool." Oh no; he believes in God like multiple millions do today. His confession combined with his actions reveals the genuineness of his heart: I believe in God, but I have lived as if He did not exist. I have lived as if there were no day of reckoning.

Not only does the soul derive its origin from God and belong to God, it needs to be saved in order to spend eternity with God. "*Receive with meekness the engrafted word, which is able to save your souls… Receiving the end of your faith, even the salvation of your souls*" (James 1:21; 1 Peter 1:9).

The rich man's death was sudden and unexpected. He thought he had a long life of ease ahead of him, but God had different plans: *"Tonight thy soul shall be required of thee, then whose shall those things be, which thou hast provided. So is he that layeth up treasures for himself, and is not rich toward God."*

What are your plans? Are you preparing for a long life? Have you included God in those plans? What are the desires of your soul? Is it the things of God or the things of this world? Have you pondered eternity?

If not, ponder this question: *"For what shall it profit a man, if he shall gain the whole world, and lose his own soul? Or what shall a man give in exchange for his soul?"* (Mark 8:36–37).

The decision must be made now. After death, it will be too late.

The Shadow

> *Yea, though I walk through the valley of the*
> *shadow of death, I will fear no evil: for thou art*
> *with me; thy rod and thy staff they comfort me.*
> —Psalms 23:4

Shadows can be scary for little children. I remember when my daughter was a little girl. She hadn't been in bed very long when she saw a shadow in her room and was frightened. The shadow looked like long bony fingers on the wall. I showed her and explained that it was the neighbor's outside light shining through the trees in the yard and casting their images on her bedroom wall. Once she understood the source and that a shadow could not hurt you, she went to sleep.

Now the twenty-third Psalm must be taken completely in the context it is written. It addresses the child of God only and cannot be applied to the unsaved individual.

For the Christian, David compares death to that of walking through a shadow. Now in order to have a shadow, light must be present. Jesus is that light in "the valley of the shadow of death." And this can only mean that the child of God is never alone and all is well with his or her soul.

However, how dark must be the way of death for the unsaved. How painful, fearful, and lonely death must be to them. It is not the shadow but death itself that greets the unbeliever. Death has no pity on them and it is eternal.

This is not the case for the Christian. We don't walk alone, nor do we walk with an inexperienced One. Jesus has walked this path before me. He has tasted death for every man. He is the One who liveth, and was dead, and behold, I am alive forevermore, Amen. He has the keys of hell and of death (Hebrews 2:9; Revelation 1:17–18).

There is no need to hurry through nor fear anything in the valley because the substance of death has been removed. Jesus has through His death, burial, and resurrection removed:

1. The Sting of Death

    "O death, where is thy sting? O grave, where is thy victory? The sting of death is sin; and the strength of sin is the law. But thanks be to God, which giveth us the victory through our Lord Jesus Christ" (1 Corinthians 15:55–57).

2. The Fear of Death

    "Forasmuch then as the children are partakers of flesh and blood, he also himself likewise took part of the same; that through death he might destroy him that had the power of death, that is, the devil; And deliver them who through fear of death were all their lifetime subject to bondage" (Hebrews 2:14–15).

3. The Power of Death

> *"Jesus said unto her, I am the resurrection and the life: he that believeth in me, though he were dead, yet shall he live. And whosoever liveth and believeth in me shall never die"* (John 11:25–26, 5:28–29).

Only the "shadow of death" is left. Every unknown of death by humanity is known by the Saviour. Every fear has been conquered, every gorge has been crossed, and every enemy has been banished because the Saviour walks with me. *"Then spake Jesus again unto them, saying, I am the light of the world: he that followeth me shall not walk in darkness, but shall have the light of life"* (John 8:12).

> *"Marvel not at this: for the hour is coming, in the which all that are in the graves shall hear his voice, And shall come forth; they that have done good, unto the resurrection of life; and they that have done evil, unto the resurrection of damnation"* (John 5:28–29).

There is nothing that can separate the believer from his Saviour: not death, life, angels, principalities, powers, things present, things to come, height, depth, nor any creature shall be able to separate us from the love of God, which is in Christ Jesus (Romans 8: 35–39).

The promise in Psalm 23—*"Yea, though I walk through the valley of the shadow of death, I will fear no evil: for thou art with me; thy rod and thy staff they comfort me"*—is to the believer alone. The unsaved have absolutely no one to walk with them through "the valley of death." They will enter the valley in the blackness of night, face the horrors of death all alone, and be separated from all that is good forever.

It's Precious

Precious in the sight of the Lord
is the death of his saints.
— Psalm 116:15

The older we get, the more we understand value: the value of time, family, friends, and even life itself. As children, we did not understand value, but we did understand "that's mine." When we entered into the teenage years, we wished away time and just could not wait to get our driver's license. Then as young adults out on our own: friends over family, my outlook on life over parental training, and the now over the future. Finally, when we reach the twilight years, for some unknown reason, we begin to understand what was really valuable or "precious" all along.

How strange and eerie it feels when we find ourselves thinking, saying, and evaluating the same things the way our parents did. For some, that wisdom comes very late in life.

A friend of mine, whom I led to the Lord a few months before his death, told me this: "It took me thirty years to hear what my father told me." As far as he was concerned, his dad had an upside-down view of life. How much heartache and tragedy he would have been spared if he had listened to his parents.

One might wonder upon reading this verse: does God have an upside-down view of death? No. I think those of us who know the Lord understand that it is us who are upside down in our view of death. What we see as a tragedy, especially in the death of a Christian, God sees as precious in His sight.

How is it precious to Him?

First, we must remember the effect of Adam's sin in the Garden of Eden. His sin resulted in the whole of humanity being separated from God.

All we like sheep have gone astray; we have
turned every one to his own way. (Isaiah 53:6)

> *There is none righteous... there is* none *that seeketh after the Lord..., there is none that doeth good..., for all have sinned and come short of the glory of God.* (Romans 3:10–12, 23)

Second, though man sinned against God, God still loved him and desired to have fellowship with him. Nevertheless, our sins came between us and God. God's holiness and righteousness demands that sin be punished without fail.

> *For the wages of sin is death.* (Romans 6:23)

> *The soul that sinneth, it shall die.* (Ezekiel 18:20)

> *But your iniquities have separated between you and your God, and your sins have hid his face from you, that he will not hear.* (Isaiah 59:2)

God does love mankind with an unconditional love (John 3:16). However, His love cannot trump His holiness, righteousness, and justice. The penalty for sin must be collected, and death is the only payment God would accept.

Third, this is where the Lord Jesus Christ comes in. Someone must die to satisfy God's righteous demand as payment for sin. Either we must die and be separated from God in the lake of fire forever, or someone could die in our place. A substitute, someone in the place of you and me.

If there were ever anyone who understood a substitute, it would have been Barabbas (Luke 23:16–25). He was guilty and Jesus was innocent. Nevertheless, Jesus took his place on an old rugged cross. It was there on that cross that Jesus, the Just for the unjust, bleed and died to pay a debt He did not owe.

This is God's only begotten Son we're talking about. He shed His blood as the payment for our sins. His blood, His blood alone, is the only payment that can atone for your sins and mine. Jesus paid the ransom God demanded for the penalty of our sins. *"Who gave himself a ransom for all, to be testified in due time"* (1 Timothy 2:6).

There has been and will never be any other means by which our sins could be paid. If there were any other way, why did Jesus die? Why was His blood shed on Calvary? There's only one answer: no other "currency" would God the Father accept as payment for our sins.

Listen, *"Forasmuch as ye know that ye were not redeemed with corruptible things, as silver and gold... But with the precious blood of Christ, as of a lamb without blemish and without spot: Who verily was foreordained before the foundation of the world"* (1 Peter 1:18–20).

"Unto him that loved us, and washed us from our sins in his own blood" (Revelation 1:5).

My friend, this is the reason God sees the death of His saints as something precious. Each and every one has been washed from their sins by the *precious blood* of His Son Jesus Christ.

The songwriter Robert Lowry asked, "What can wash away my sins, What can make me whole again?" And then he answers, "Nothing but the blood of Jesus."

Have you been to Jesus for the cleansing power? Are you washed in the blood of the Lamb? If not, you need to be in order for your death to be *precious in His sight.*

The Last Enemy

> *The last enemy that shall be destroyed is death.*
> —1 Corinthians 15:26

Death, what a tyrant it is. It has neither conscience nor regard as to its victims whether they are in the womb, young, or elderly. Death has no morals. It shows no mercy whether you are righteous or wicked. Death has no financial obligations. It cares not whether you are rich or poor, have good credit, bad credit, or bankrupt. Death has no boundaries. You can run but you can't hide.

Death has wreaked havoc since its inception. It has caused more heartache and heartbreak than we care to remember and will continue until the day it is destroyed. There is only one good thing that could be said about death—it has consistently done its job for thousands of years.

As a matter of fact, death has claimed and incarcerated all of its victims but two. From the creation to this present moment, only two people have escaped the jaws of death: Enoch and Elijah (Genesis 5:21–24; 2 Kings 2:1–11).

Now it's not uncommon for people to question why God has allowed death or even to blame God for the death of a loved one. The reason being they do not understand the origin of death.

God is not the author of death. Life originated with God (Genesis 1, 2). And God *"breathed into his nostrils the breath of life; and man became a living soul"* (Genesis 2:7). Jesus said, *"I am come that they might have life, and that they might have it more abundantly"* (John 10:10). And not just physical life but eternal life as well: *"And this is the record, that God hath given to us eternal life, and this life is in his Son. He that hath the Son hath life; and he that hath not the Son of God hath not life"* (1 John 5:11–12).

Death, as previously discussed, is the consequence of sin. If Adam had not sinned, there would be no death. Remember, *"Wherefore, as by one man sin entered into the world, and death by sin; and so death passed upon all men, for that all have sinned"* (Romans 5:12).

The blame lies squarely on Adam's shoulders. God cannot be blamed. Neither can Satan, though he is not blameless. It was Satan who *deceived* Eve in the Garden, but Adam knowingly and willfully disobeyed God's command (1 Timothy 2:13–15; Genesis 2:17).

His disobedience opened the floodgate to all death: mankind and all of nature. Nevertheless, according to the Word of God, death will be destroyed, not annihilated but it will lose its power.

It is true that Jesus has the *"keys of hell and of death"* (Revelation 1:18). However, He did not render death ineffective. God's program concerning death was progressive, not immediate destruction. Why? Sin against an eternal God demands eternal consequences. The "last enemy" to be destroyed is for the believer alone. Please allow me to try and explain.

In the Garden of Eden, the *consequences* of sin were announced by God to Adam: death (Genesis 2:17). Throughout Scripture, the *remedy* for death was given. Isaiah 9:6 says, "*A child is born and a son is given.* This Son is none other than Jesus; Who came to taste death for every man" (Hebrews 2:9, 15). Death was *officially* defeated when Jesus died on the cross for our sins, was buried and rose again the third day *according to the scriptures* (1 Corinthians 15:1–4). "*Knowing that Christ being raised from the dead dieth no more; death hath no more dominion over him. For in that he died, he died unto sin once, but in that he liveth, he liveth unto God*" (Romans 6:9–10). Though death has continued to claim its victims since Jesus officially defeated it on the cross, the *actuality and finality* of death for the saved will be fully implemented in eternity (Revelation 21:1–5). "*And I saw a new heaven and a new earth… And I heard a great voice out of heaven saying… And God shall wipe away all tears from their eyes; and there shall be no more death… for the former things are passed away… Behold, I make all things new.*"

However, the same is not true for the unsaved. They will be incarcerated and forever quarantined, existing in a *state of eternal death*. Meaning, they will be separated from God in the lake of fire forever.

> *And the sea gave up the dead which were in it; death and hell delivered up the dead which were in them… And death and hell were cast into the lake of fire. This is the second death. And whosoever was not found written in the book of life was cast into the lake of fire.* (Revelation 21:13–15)
>
> *And the smoke of their torment ascendeth up for ever and ever: they have no rest day nor night.* (Revelation 14:11)

And many of them that sleep in the dust of the
earth shall awake, some to everlasting life, and some
to shame and everlasting contempt. (Daniel 12:2)

And shall come forth; they that have done
good, unto the resurrection of life; and they that
have done evil, unto the resurrection f damnation.
(John 5:29)

Death has been conquered by Christ, and His victory is to all
who will receive His gift of life. All will face physical death; however,
only the unsaved will experience eternal death.

As Sleep

These things said he: and after that he saith
unto them, Our friend Lazarus sleepeth; but
I go, that I may wake him out of sleep. Then
said his disciples, Lord, if he sleep, he shall
do well. Howbeit Jesus spake of his death.
—John 11:11–13

"Sleep," what an illustration for the believer. Albert Barnes said,
"It is a beautiful and tender expression: removing all that is dreadful
in death, and filling the mind with the idea of calm repose after a life
of toil."

Do you remember the children's prayer? "Now I lay me down
to sleep, I pray the Lord my soul to keep, and if I die before I wake, I
pray the Lord my soul to take: Amen." Parents taught their children
this prayer as a reminder of Who watched over and kept them all
night long.

Jesus compares death to taking a permanent rest from the toils
of life. He was aware of Lazarus's sickness. He knew it would lead to
his death if he did not heal him. However, he waited two days and

Lazarus died. Herein is the beauty of the passage. Jesus did not send his disciples to raise Lazarus from the dead; Jesus personally came.

As a child, many can remember momma tucking you in, kissing you good night, and saying things will be better in the morning. In the morning, it was her gentle voice, touch, and smiling face that greeted you. She was right: all the hurt, pains, and disappointments of yesterday are far behind as you face a brand-new day.

In like manner, we rest in this promise: "*For the Lord himself shall descend from heaven with a shout, with the voice of the archangel, and the trump of God: and the dead in Christ shall rise first:... Wherefore comfort one another with these words*" (1 Thessalonians 5:16, 18).

So shall it be when it comes our time to die? We will close our eyes to all the ills of this life; we will face a brand-new day and see the smiling face of our Lord and Saviour Jesus Christ.

No Pleasure

Say unto them, As I live saith the Lord God,
I have no pleasure in the death of the wicked;
but that the wicked turn from his way and
live: turn ye, turn ye from your evil ways;
for why will ye die, O house of Israel?
—Ezekiel 33:11

Recently, a lady came to me and made this comment: "*No one goes to hell anymore.*" The statement did not surprise me, nor did I disagree with it. I understood the reason behind why she said it. She had attended several funerals and read the obituaries; not one thing was said about hell and everyone had gone home to be with the Lord.

However, I was surprised that this statement came from an unsaved person, one who has attended a church where hell was preached, who admitted to being under conviction from the message. Nevertheless, she has not repented of her sin and trusted Jesus as her Saviour.

Have you ever been to a funeral and heard these words? "We are gathered here today to honor the memory and life of _____. He is survived by his wife _____ of _____ years, His two sons _____and _____. One daughter _____ and her husband_____ and their twin children _____ and _____. However, I stand before you this day with a broken heart, not for those who have survived, but for _____, because he is in hell today!"

I think the answer is never! Nevertheless, the statement would be true in every case where the deceased did not receive the Lord Jesus Christ as Saviour. However, it would not be well received by family and friends. Many would find it distasteful, offensive, and unpleasant. Some would accuse the speaker of being insensitive and judgmental. Others would opt for deathbed repentance saying, "He could have asked God for forgiveness before he died." Many of you reading this book would be highly offended if such a statement was made about your loved one.

The intensity of that offense, which would boil and overflow with words of disapproval, pales in light of God's displeasure *"in the death of the wicked."* God is not sadistic but pleads for the unsaved person *to turn from his way and live.* Neither is God soft on sin: *"Turn ye from your evil ways; for why will ye die?* God is not unfair: *"Behold I set before this day a blessing and a curse; A blessing, if ye obey… And a curse if ye will not obey"* (Deuteronomy 11:26–28).

God is not willing that any perish but that all come to repentance (2 Peter 3:9). God is omniscient; He knows and reveals in His word what the unsaved will experience for all eternity:

- Unending thirst (Luke 16:24)
- Unquenchable fire (Mark 9:43–48)
- Unsuppressed memory (Luke 16:25)
- Unending screams (Matthew 13:42)
- Utter darkness (Matthew 22:13)
- Unending suffering (Revelation 14:11)

He knows the unsaved will exist in an eternal state of torment. Even though God loves the world, does this mean everybody goes to heaven when they die? No! God's love for all humanity is stated in John 3:16 and it is proven in Romans 5:8. However, His love cannot trump His justice. Sin must be punished: *the soul that sinneth, it shall die* (Ezekiel 18:4). "Jesus was punished and die for our sins on Calvary."

> *For he hath made him to be sin for us, who knew no sin; that we might be made the righteousness of God in him.* (1 Corinthians 5:21)

> *For Christ also hath once suffered for sins, the just for the unjust, that he might bring us to God, being put to death in the flesh, but quickened by the Spirit.* (1 Peter 3:18)

God did all He could at Calvary to keep every soul out of hell. Therefore, the person who rejects Jesus Christ as their Saviour will be cast into the lake of fire, but know for certain, God takes no pleasure in the death of the wicked.

Questions Concerning Death

There is probably no subject that has generated more questions than the subject of death. Equally so, this subject has generated even more false ideas or speculations. Some of those ideas are meant to comfort the hearts of the bereaved, while others are given to stifle the thoughts of accountability to God. Yet whatever the motive behind the consolation, many of those statements are based on ignorance, not facts.

Perhaps these examples will suffice for the moment. You have probably heard this statement given after the death of a child: "*God needed another angel, so He took*_____." Those words may be comforting to a mom and dad whose child has died unexpectedly, but it is far, far from the truth. More on this a little later.

This comment is often made after a long battle with cancer or a debilitating disease. "They are not suffering anymore; they're in a better place." This statement can only be true if the person who died was a Christian. If not, then his or her suffering has intensified and will now be eternal.

It will be impossible to address every question because I have not heard them all. With the help of other preachers and the questions I have been presented with, perhaps we can answer most of them. At the same time, we will try to address some of those false statements made concerning death.

Where Are the Dead?

There are those who teach the dead are in the grave and the soul is asleep. Therefore, the dead are unconscious and inactive, waiting for the resurrection. Also, there are others who say death is the cessation of life altogether. Are either of this true?

The supporting verse for such teaching is found in Ecclesiastes 3:19–20: "*For that which befalleth the sons of men befalleth beast; even one thing befalleth them: as one dieth, so dieth the other; yea, they have all one breath; so that a man hath no preeminence above the beast: for all is vanity. All go unto one place; all are of the dust, and all turn to dust again.*"

If this was the only verse in the Bible concerning death, then it would seem logical that death is the cessation of life. The death of the body, whether man or beast, is the same. You can speak to a dead loved one and never get an answer. You could call your dead pet by name a hundred times, and it would never respond. You could even hit, slap, or kick that person or pet; they would never feel the blows nor respond in any manner. Why? The body is dead to all feelings. Therefore, the scripture is right in saying, "*As one dieth, so dieth the other.*"

But the proponents of this teaching fail to take this scripture in context. One must understand the viewpoint from which Ecclesiastes is written. The key phrase in this wonderful book is "*Under the sun.*" In other words, Ecclesiastes is written from man's point of view, not God's. Yes, if we were to happen upon a fatal accident in which a man and his dog were killed, neither would respond no matter how hard the paramedics tried. They would both be lifeless, motionless, and pronounced dead at the scene. They would both be buried and from man's viewpoint "*as one dieth, so dieth the other.*"

But what does God say about the matter? For the answer, let's observe four passages of scripture. The first is found in Revelation 6:9–11.

> *⁹And when he had opened the fifth seal, I saw under the altar the souls of them that were slain for the word of God, and for the testimony which they held:*

> *[10]And they cried with a loud voice, saying,
> How long, O Lord, holy and true, dost thou not
> judge and avenge our blood on them that dwell on
> the earth?*
>
> *[11]And white robes were given unto every one of
> them; and it was said unto them, that they should
> rest yet for a little season, until their fellowservants
> also and their brethren, that should be killed as they
> were, should be fulfilled.*

In Revelation 6, God pulls back the curtain and allows us to look into heaven at those who have died because of their faith in Christ Jesus. Notice that is said of them, *"They cried with a loud voice,"* which would be impossible if soul sleep or the cessation of life is true.

Next, it is said of them, *"How long, O Lord, holy and true, dost thou not judge and avenge our blood on them that dwell on the earth?"* This statement gives further evidence of life after death. First, they remembered how they died: *"avenge our blood."* They are reminding God that their death was not a natural or accidental death but deliberate murder. Second, they know their murderers are still alive: *"that dwell on the earth."* This further refutes soul sleep and cessation of life whenever someone dies.

In Luke 16:19–31, God again opens the hatch and allows us to gaze into the regions of the damned in order to see what's going on with those who died without Christ.

> *[19]There was a certain rich man, which was
> clothed in purple and fine linen, and fared sumptu-
> ously every day:*
>
> *[20]And there was a certain beggar named
> Lazarus, which was laid at his gate, full of sores,*
>
> *[21]And desiring to be fed with the crumbs
> which fell from the rich man's table: moreover the
> dogs came and licked his sores.*

²²And it came to pass, that the beggar died, and was carried by the angels into Abraham's bosom: the rich man also died, and was buried;

²³And in hell he lift up his eyes, being in torments, and seeth Abraham afar off, and Lazarus in his bosom.

²⁴And he cried and said, Father Abraham, have mercy on me, and send Lazarus, that he may dip the tip of his finger in water, and cool my tongue; for I am tormented in this flame.

²⁵But Abraham said, Son, remember that thou in thy lifetime receivedst thy good things, and likewise Lazarus evil things: but now he is comforted, and thou art tormented.

²⁶And beside all this, between us and you there is a great gulf fixed: so that they which would pass from hence to you cannot; neither can they pass to us, that would come from thence.

²⁷Then he said, I pray thee therefore, father, that thou wouldest send him to my father's house:

²⁸For I have five brethren; that he may testify unto them, lest they also come into this place of torment.

²⁹Abraham saith unto him, They have Moses and the prophets; let them hear them.

³⁰And he said, Nay, father Abraham: but if one went unto them from the dead, they will repent.

³¹And he said unto him, If they hear not Moses and the prophets, neither will they be persuaded, though one rose from the dead.

The scene before us is not one of joy, by any means. It describes in living color what is happening to an individual who dies and goes to hell. It is a disturbing passage to many people, and I can understand why one would readily accept soul sleep and cessation of life. Yet one's belief, opinion, or preference cannot change or alter the Word of God.

Listen to the evidence God gives concerning both men: Lazarus and the rich man. They both died (verse 22). However, more is said about the rich man in this passage of scripture, so we will focus on him. In this life, we have what is known as the five senses: seeing, hearing, tasting, touching, and smelling. It is a fact that one does not have to possess all five of these in order to be considered alive. But a careful examination of Luke 16 reveals that this rich man, whom God said was dead, possessed all five.

- He could feel—*"being in torments"* (verse 23)
- He could see—*"seeth Abraham afar off"* (verse 23)
- He could taste—*"that he may dip the tip of his finger in water"* (verse 24)
- He could hear—*"But Abraham said, Son"* (verse 25)
- He could smell—*"I am tormented in this flame"* (verse 24)

The key words in Luke 16 are found in verse 23: *"being in."* The word *being* means existing in a continual state or condition. These two men died and are now in two separate places, existing forever in two different environments. This is impossible if Ecclesiastes is teaching death from God's perspective.

The third passage we will look into is Luke 9:27–33:

> *28And it came to pass about an eight days after these sayings, he took Peter and John and James, and went up into a mountain to pray.*
>
> *29And as he prayed, the fashion of his countenance was altered, and his raiment was white and glistering.*
>
> *30And, behold, there talked with him two men, which were Moses and Elias:*
>
> *31Who appeared in glory, and spake of his decease which he should accomplish at Jerusalem.*
>
> *32But Peter and they that were with him were heavy with sleep: and when they were awake, they saw his glory, and the two men that stood with him.*

³³And it came to pass, as they departed from him, Peter said unto Jesus, Master, it is good for us to be here: and let us make three tabernacles; one for thee, and one for Moses, and one for Elias: not knowing what he said.

Note the two people who are named Moses and Elias or Elijah. These two men lived hundreds of years before Peter, James, and John were ever born. In verse 31, they spoke to Jesus about His upcoming crucifixion.

Again, this is impossible if soul sleep and cessation of life at death is true. Now for the final passage of scripture:

"I say unto you, that likewise joy shall be in heaven over one sinner that repenteth, more than over ninety and nine persons, which need no repentance… Likewise, I say unto you, there is joy in the presence of the angels of God over one sinner that repenteth" (Luke 15:7, 10).

Who could these be who are *"in the presence of the angels of God"*? They could only be the saints who have died and gone on before us. The Bible says they are aware of sinners who repent of their sins and trust Christ as their Saviour.

I believe these four passages of scripture are ample proof that those who have died still exist in heaven or hell and that they are conscious, not sleeping in the grave. Also, these scripture references provide the answers to several more questions.

Are the Dead Conscious of What Is Happening on Earth?

In our first scripture reference, Revelation 6:10, those who were murdered for their faith knew their assailants were still alive and that God had not judged them. How much they knew seems to be limited, for God told them that others would die like they had before He would take vengeance on the perpetrators.

Then in Luke 16:27–28, the rich man knew he had five brothers who were still alive, and he knew their lifestyles would lead them to "this place of torment" if they did not repent.

Again in Luke 15:7, 10, those in heaven are aware of every sinner who repents and expresses great joy when they witness such an occasion. But do those in heaven know when a person dies and goes to hell? I can't be dogmatic about it, but it seems possible. In Revelation 21:4 it reads, "*And God shall wipe away all tears from their eyes.*" A careful study of this section of scripture reveals that God does not wipe away our tears until time is no more and eternity begins. It is very possible the saints in glory are aware of loved ones who die and go to hell. If the rich man in hell knew his brothers were headed there and that Lazarus was in Paradise, are the saints in heaven more ignorant than he?

Hebrews 12:1 says, "*Wherefore seeing we also are compassed about with so great a cloud of witnesses, let us lay aside every weight and the sin which doth so easily beset us.*" The "witnesses" in this verse refers to those in chapter 11, and all those saints died a few thousand years ago.

How much they know is not clearly stated. However, there is ample evidence that the dead have some knowledge, though they are not omniscient. Even Moses and Elijah in Luke 9:31 knew that Jesus's death was imminent.

Will We Know One Another?

Yes. Back in Luke 16:24, the rich man recognized Abraham even though he had never personally met him. He also remembered Lazarus. We read in Luke 9:30–32 where Peter and John recognized Moses and Elijah when they were on the Mount of Transfiguration.

In 1 Corinthians 13:12, it reads, "*For now we see through a glass darkly; but then face to face: now we know in part; but then shall I know even as also I am known.*"

Dr. Harold Sightler says, "Allow me to suggest that surely we shall not know less over there than here. We can rest assured that we will know our dear loved ones when we meet around the throne of God."

The rich man recognized Lazarus. Peter and John recognized Moses and Elijah. Therefore, it seems evident that God will permit us to retain our personal identities.

Will We Remember Our Lives on Earth?

From the evidence presented in scripture, the answer is yes. The rich man in hell was called upon to *"remember that thou in thy lifetime receivedest thy good things, and likewise Lazarus evil things: but now he is comforted and thou art tormented."* He remembers his five brothers who were still alive. However, he doesn't mention his parents. Why? It is possible they died before him and were Christians and already in heaven. It is also possible they were still alive and believers. However, he knew his brothers were not, that they were following his lifestyle and would end up in hell with him (Luke 16:25, 28).

Likewise in Revelation 6:10, those who had been murdered remembered how they died, and the ones who killed them. Before I leave this question, I'd like for us to ponder the power of the mind to recall events of the past. Our memory can be a source of blessing or of great sorrow.

Previously, I asked if those in heaven would know if a loved one died and went to hell. I also said that I can't be dogmatic; nevertheless, it is possible. Revelation 21:4 says God shall wipe away all tears from their eyes, and this happens when time is no more.

Someone asked: How could that be heaven if we can remember that our loved ones are in hell for all eternity? Listen to the word God: *"For the former things are passed away... Behold, I make all things new"* (Revelation 21:4–5). When earth is no longer and time is no more, God will remove the memory of former things from the minds of His children. Unfortunately, that will not be the case for the unsaved who spend eternity in hell. The memory will be a source of torment for ever. They will remember every opportunity they had to get saved, but like the rich, they saw no need of God's salvation. "*Son, remember*" (Luke 16:25).

Do They Have Any Emotions?

Yes. "*There is joy in the presence of the angels of God over one sinner that repenteth.*" John the apostle was caught up into heaven in Revelation 5:4, and he wept much when there was no one found in heaven or earth worthy to open the seven-sealed book.

In Matthew 22:13, Jesus says, "*Bind him hand and foot, and take him away, and cast him into outer darkness; there shall be weeping and gnashing of teeth.*"

Revelation 4–5 is filled with those in heaven praising, worshiping, and singing unto the "Lamb" that liveth for ever and ever.

When we come to Revelation 8:1, we read, "*And when he had opened the seventh seal, there was silence in heaven about the space of half hour.*" The saints stood in utter shock at the sight that was transpiring before their eyes. So I think it is safe to say they have emotions.

Will There Be Any Babies in Heaven or Hell?

First of all, no one goes to hell except those who reject Jesus Christ as their Saviour. Infants and older children who are incapable of distinguishing between right and wrong are sheltered by the mercy, grace, and the blood of the Lord Jesus Christ. This would also include adults who are mentally challenged.

In 2 Samuel 12:1–23, the infant child of King David dies, revealing the truth about infant deaths. In verses 22–23, we read, "*And he said, While the child was yet alive, I fasted and wept: for I said, Who can tell whether God will be gracious to me, that the child may live. But now he is dead, wherefore should I fast? Can I bring him back again? I shall go to him, but he shall not return to me.*" Hebrews 11:32 clearly states that David is in heaven. Since David said, "*I shall go to him,*" then the child is in heaven.

Do they remain babies? John MacArthur said, "Will there be strollers in the New Jerusalem? No. Whatever their limitations are here, whatever their imperfections are here, whatever their immaturities are here; they aren't there."

MacArthur shares three passages of scripture to support his answer. I will share two of them. In 1 John 3:2, the Bible tells us that "*it doth not yet appear what we shall be: but we know that, when he [Jesus Christ] shall appear, we shall be like him; for we shall see him as he is.*" This verse does not state how old we will be in heaven, but it does say we will be like Jesus. Jesus is no longer the baby of Bethlehem. So I think it will be safe to say there will be no infants in heaven.

The second and the most compelling passage is found in Revelation 7:9–10: "*After this I beheld, and, lo, a great multitude, which no man could number, of all nations, and kindreds, and people, and tongues, stood before the throne, and before the Lamb, clothed with white robes and palms in their hands; And cried with a loud voice, saying, Salvation to our God which sitteth upon the throne, and unto the Lamb.*" Here is compelling evidence that the mentally challenged, the aborted child, and the infants who die prematurely will not remain that way in heaven.

Behold a great multitude "*stood*" before the throne. It is impossible for the aborted child, the victim of crib death, or one just a few months old to be standing before the throne. Next, they have "*palms in their hands.*" Babies are incapable of holding palm branches and waving them in praise to the Father and the Son. Finally, they "*cried with a loud voice.*" Yes, babies can cry, and very loudly at times, but it is unintelligible. Here, their words were intelligible, and it implies they understood what they were saying.

I think scriptures provide ample proof there are no infants in heaven.

Do All Suicide Victims Go to Hell?

No. This is contrary to the opinions of many. The normal response to a suicide victim is, "You know where they are!" And the *where*, is always hell. How biblical is that response?

May I quote a pastor friend of mine, John Keeter? While preaching the funeral of a young lady who had committed suicide, he made this statement: "Her eternal destiny was not determined by her death but by her faith."

The idea that one immediately goes to hell upon committing suicide is based on the misunderstanding of salvation. Salvation is totally and completely of God. Salvation is by grace, and *all* our sins are completely *blotted out* by the finished work of Jesus Christ on the cross.

> *"And you, being dead in your sins and the uncircumcision of your flesh, hath he quickened together with him, having forgiven you all trespasses; Blotting out the handwriting of ordinances that was against us, which was contrary to us, and took it out of the way, nailing it to his cross; And having spoiled principalities and powers, he made a shew of them openly, triumphing over them in it"* (Colossians 2:13–15).

The Word of God teaches that *all* Christians' sins are *forgiven* when they come to Christ by faith. What does God mean by *having forgiven you all trespasses?* He means exactly what He said—*all*. Here's the beauty of the grace of God. God forgives me of *all* my past sins, my present sins, and my future sins.

Sounds impossible? How could God forgive the sins I have yet to commit? May I ask you this question: In relationship to Christ's death on the cross, where were you? Were you living before He came and died? Were you present at the cross when He died? Or did you come after His death, burial, resurrection, and ascension? There is only one answer. We came after Christ's death and ascension, therefore, making all our sins in the future. When Jesus died, He died *once for all*, and by His death, He obtained *eternal redemption* for the believer (Hebrews 10:10, 9:10).

Still sounds impossible? It does from a human viewpoint. However, God is not a man (Numbers 23:19). God is omniscient— all knowing. He knew you before you were born. He knows everything you will say, think, or do. He knows your needs before you ask, and nothing in all creation is hidden from Him (Jeremiah 1:4–8; Psalm 139:1–6; Matthew 6:8; Hebrews 4:13). He already knows how and when you will die (John 21:18–19; 2 Peter 1:12–13; Revelation 6:6–11; 1 Kings 21:17–19; 2 Kings 22:34–39).

The victim of a suicide is a mystery and surprise to the survivors, but not to God. He knew beforehand both the how and the why the believer took their life.

The reason people say suicide victims go to hell is that suicide is *self-murder.* Therefore, since murder is a sin and they were not able to confess that sin before they died, they went to hell. These precious people have the idea that salvation is based on good works instead of grace. Christians are saved by grace, and they are kept by grace.

If our entrance into heaven is based on the confession of our sins, then none of us would make it. Why? Can you remember every sin you ever committed? And if you could remember all of them, what about the sins of omission? God said in James 4:17, "*Therefore to him that knoweth to do good, and doeth it not, to him it is sin.*"

Therefore, if the suicide victim went to hell because they were unable to confess that sin before death, then consider this.

1. A Christian is driving down the road, sees a very attractive individual of the opposite sex, and has an adulterous thought. While infatuated with that thought, they cross the center line, hit an oncoming car head on, and die instantly without asking God's forgiveness. Does that person go to hell also?

2. Suppose you go to bed tonight and you are angry or bitter toward your neighbor or mate. Suppose you die suddenly of a heart attack before you can confess it to God and get

right with your neighbor or mate. Will you go to hell as well?

3. Lastly, suppose you accidentally hit someone's car in the parking lot, doing some minor damage. You know that the right thing to do is to find the owner or leave a note with your contact information on it, but you are in a hurry, and it is just a minor scratch. So you leave the scene, never mention it to anyone, and die without getting it right with God or the owner. Do you go to hell also?

You will, if going to heaven is based on you confessing your sins before you die! The list is endless, and I doubt there's ever been an individual who died without some unconfessed sin. Entrance into heaven is not based on the confession of sins; it based on confessing to God that I am a sinner and receiving Jesus Christ as my Saviour, Who died for *all* my sins! To God, suicide, adultery, bitterness, and not doing the right thing are all sins.

Another reason people say Christians who commit suicide can't go to heaven is that they have committed the "unpardonable sin." In Matthew 12:22–31, God defines the unpardonable sin, and suicide does not fit that description. As a matter of fact, no Christian can commit this sin, only the unsaved can.

My friend, don't worry if your loved one or friend was a Christian and committed suicide. Their death did not determine their eternity; their faith in Christ did. Nevertheless, if the suicide victim was unsaved, that individual did go to hell. However, it was not because he or she took their life but because they had rejected Jesus Christ as their Saviour!

Do We Become Angels When We Die?

The answer is no. I know people mean well when they say, "The Lord needed another angel," but how scriptural is that saying? The truth is angels are created beings, even before humanity. Nonetheless, there is absolutely nothing found in the Bible that indicates they were formerly human beings (Job 38: 4–7 "sons of God"; Colossians 1:15–17).

Angels are entirely different from humans:

1. Hebrews 2:5–8 tells us that man was created inferior to the angels.
2. Hebrews 1:13–14 reveals they are spirits and the ministers of God: agents to carry out the plan of God and to minister to those who follow Christ.
3. First Peter 1:12 describes their interest in the Gospel. Why such an interest in the Gospel if they were humans before they died? Salvation by grace would be the very reason they are in heaven, not a mystery that is unfamiliar to them.

There are five reasons why we do not become angels upon death:

1. Genesis 1:26–27 reveals in whose image man was created. Adam was created in the image and likeness of God, not the angels.
2. First Corinthians 15:49 further explains that as we have borne the image of the earthly, we shall also bear the image of the heavenly. And just in case someone may apply that verse to the angels, 1 John 3:1–2 clarifies whose image that will be. The "He" in verse 2 is the Lord Jesus Christ: "*When he shall appear, we shall be like him; for we shall see him as he is.*"
3. Philippians 3:20–21 describes our present body as "*our vile body.*" When Jesus comes, He will change that body into one "*fashioned like unto his glorious body,*" not into that of angels.
4. Matthew 17:1–4 records the events and persons on the Mount of Transfiguration. Peter, James, and John accompanied Jesus to the top of the mount and there appeared unto them Moses and Elijah. These two men had died and when they appeared to Jesus and His disciples. They appeared as men, not angels.

5. Finally, in 1 Thessalonians 3:13 and 2 Thessalonians 1:7, there is a clear distinction made between the angels and the saints when the Lord Jesus Christ comes again. *"At the coming of our Lord Jesus Christ with his saints... when the Lord Jesus shall be revealed from heaven with his mighty angels."*

Conclusion: Angels and humanity are two distinct and separate beings. Therefore, we can say without reservation that people do not become angels upon death no matter how sweet that sounds.

What about Reincarnation?

Reincarnation is a popular belief among the Hindus. It is the belief that those who die will live again in some other form of life whether human, animal, or insect. Its concept implies that the human soul is eternal as it strives for perfection and becomes one with the divine.

This concept offers humanity multiple opportunities to get things right with the Creator, God. It has no biblical footing at all. While Jesus was on the cross, He told the repentant thief: *"To day shalt thou be with me in paradise"* (Luke 23:42). Jesus did not say that he would have another chance at life, which is an appealing concept when one comes down to the end of life and realizes "I've blown it!"

However appealing the concept is, we find nothing in the Bible to support this doctrine. Jesus said to the rich fool, *"Thou fool, this night thy soul shall be required of thee: then whose shall those things be, which thou hast provided"* (Luke 12:16–20). Jesus did not offer him a second chance in life to get it right.

Then in 2 Corinthians 5:8, *"We are confident, I say, and willing rather to be absent from the body, and to be present with the Lord."*

In Luke 16:22–23, we read, *"And it came to pass, that the beggar died, and was carried by the angel into Abraham's bosom: the rich man also died and was buried; And in hell he lift up his eyes, being in torments."*

The teaching of reincarnation has deceived billions of people who have and will realize its deception at death, but then it will be too late!

Is Purgatory Biblical?

The teaching of "purgatory" finds its origin in the Roman Catholic Church. Purgatory is an intermediate state after death where one must undergo purification to achieve the holiness required for entrance into heaven. This can be achieved by the prayers of surviving family members, taking mass and paying the priest to perform mass in their behalf.

All this denies the sufficiency of Christ's death for our sins. The idea of suffering for our sins after death contradicts everything God said Jesus accomplished on the Cross.

Isaiah 53:5 reads, "*But he [Jesus] was wounded for our transgressions, he was bruised for our iniquities: the chastisement of our peace was upon him; and with his stripes we are healed.*"

Note that this is what Jesus did for us. Now listen to God the Father's response: "*He [the Father] shall see of the travail of his [Jesus] soul and shall be* satisfied" (Isaiah 53:11).

Hebrews 10:12–14 reads, "*But this man [Jesus], after he had offered one sacrifice for sins forever, sat down on the right hand of God* [sat down denotes a completed work]. *For by one offering he hath perfected for ever them that are sanctified.*"

Hebrews 9:11–12 describes the sufficiency and longevity of Christ's death on the cross. Year after year, offerings were made, which could never take away sins nor could they perfect the sinner. Yet Jesus did not offer a lamb for sin. He gave Himself as a sacrifice for our sin, therefore obtaining what no other offering could. "*But Jesus… by his own blood he entered in once into the holy place, having obtained eternal redemption for us.*" Purgatory says I must suffer for my sin.

In the words of the songwriter George Bennard, "In the old rugged cross, stained with blood so divine, A wondrous beauty I see; For twas on that old cross Jesus suffered and died, to pardon and sanctify me. So I'll cherish the old rugged cross, Till my trophies at last I lay down; I will cling to the old rugged cross, And exchange it some day for a crown."

The beauty of the cross is that Jesus has already suffered and died for my sins: the Just for the unjust. Jesus has provided *eternal redemption* for all who place their faith in Him. Therefore, God does not require me to suffer at all for my sins.

As a matter of fact, God declares there is absolutely no judgment for the believer; both now and forever. God has spoken clearly about this matter of purgatory: "*There is therefore now no condemnation to them which are in Christ Jesus*" (Romans 8:1).

Since there is no condemnation or judgment for the believer in Christ, there is no need for purgatory and purification. Neither will there be a purgatory for the unbeliever. The unbeliever will die in his or her sins, and like the rich man in Luke 16:22–23, "*The rich man died, and was buried, And in hell he lift up his eyes, being in torments*," he or she will immediately be in hell. There will be no second chances, no purgatory, and no prayers or money offered that will grant their release.

According to the scriptures, and they are the final authority concerning death, the rich man went immediately to hell at death and Lazarus went immediately to heaven. Therefore, purgatory is not biblical.

What about Deathbed Repentance?

Deathbed repentance finds its origin in Luke's account of the crucifixion of Jesus Christ. It is the only example of genuine deathbed repentance in the entire Bible.

> *"And one of the malefactors which were hanged railed on him, saying, If thou be Christ, save thyself and us. But the other answering rebuked him, saying, Dost not thou fear God, seeing thou art in the same condemnation? And we indeed justly, for we receive the due reward of our deeds: but this man hath done nothing amiss. And he said unto Jesus, Lord, remember me when thou comest into thy kingdom. And Jesus said unto him, Verily I say unto thee, To day shalt thou be with me in paradise"*
> (Luke 23:39–43).

Is deathbed repentance or conversions genuine? Is it possible for one to come to faith in Christ and go to heaven a few hours or moments before they die? One, who before that moment

- professed no religious affiliation
- never attended church
- thought religion was for women, children, and weaklings
- used God's Name in vain with every breath
- was a murderer
- an agnostic
- a thief
- a liar
- a drunkard
- an adulterer
- and the list could go on or even an atheist

Is it possible for him or her to repent of their sins, trust Jesus as their Saviour, and go to heaven just moments before their death? Secondly, is it fair?

The answer to both questions is yes. But it comes with a price, an understanding of some facts, and a huge warning.

Understanding Some Facts

One's perception of deathbed conversions must be accompanied with the understanding of God and the means of salvation.

1.   God Is Patient and God Is Love

First Peter 3:9 reminds us that God is "*longsuffering to us-ward, not willing that any should perish, but that ALL should come to repentance.*" It is not and never has been God's desire for anyone to go to hell. Hell was created for the devil and his angels (Matthew 25:41).

First John 4:8 declares that God is love, and John 3:16–17 reveals how much God loves us. God gave His Son for us and sent Jesus into the world, not to condemn the world but that the world through him might be saved.

God is not a despot Who delights in the sufferings of the unsaved. Ezekiel 33:11 reads, "*I have no pleasure in the death of the wicked.*"

2.   God Demands Repentance and Faith

The holiness and righteousness of God cannot trump His love or His patience. In Luke 13:3, 5 Jesus says, "*I tell you, Nay: but, except ye repent, ye shall all likewise perish.*" Also in Acts 20:21, we are told, "*Testifying both to the Jews and also to the Greeks, repentance toward God, and faith toward our Lord Jesus Christ.*"

Repentance is a change of mind that results in a change of one's lifestyle. It is a change of heart and mind about oneself, sin, and God.

The Bible reveals four things about the crucifixion and those crucified with Christ:

a.   Two men were crucified with Jesus (Luke 23:32).
b.   One on the right hand and the other on the left (Luke 23:33).

c. They were thieves (Matthew 27:44).
d. Both reviled, criticized, and insulted the Lord (Mark 15:32)

However, the Gospel of Luke reveals what the other Gospels did not—the repentance. One thief said, "*If thou be Christ, saved thyself and us.*" The other thief *now* separates or distances himself from him by saying, "*Dost not thou fear God, seeing thou art in the same condemnation? And we indeed justly, for we receive the due reward for our deeds: but this man hath done nothing amiss.*"

Do you see his repentance? One moment he is reviling Jesus, angry and critical of Him. Next, you find him rebuking his partner in crime, acknowledging their guilt and defending the innocence of Christ. This is a repentance which leads to salvation.

We do not naturally view ourselves as wicked, ungodly, heathen, or guilty of sin. As a matter of fact, we would be offended and get angry if someone said we were any or all these things. We don't mind taking the middle ground: I may not be as good as _____, but I'm not as bad as _____ either. However, the truth is this: it is not how we view ourselves that is important; it is how God sees us that counts. And God sums up *all* humanity in twelve words: "*For all have sinned and come short of the glory of God*" (Romans 3:23).

Yes, it is true; God is love and patient but God also demands repentance whether you are young, middle-aged, or on your deathbed. "*Except ye repent, ye shall all likewise perish*" (Luke 13:3, 5).

God also requires faith. "*But without faith, it is impossible to please him: for he that cometh to God must believe that he is, and that he is the rewarder of them that diligently seek him*" (Hebrews 11:6).

Biblical faith is not what most people perceive it to be. The faith that pleases God is one that accepts and confesses the existence of God: "*For he that cometh to God must believe that he is.*" However, faith must also acknowledge that God is trustworthy, "*and that he is the rewarder of them that diligently seek him.*"

The repentant thief displayed his faith in Christ when he said, "*This man hath done nothing amiss.*" He acknowledged that Jesus had no sin and He was dying a substitutionary death: *the Just for the unjust* This is the first step in biblical faith. How? Only God, Jesus being God in the flesh, is good and without sin (Luke 18:18–19; 2 Corinthians 5:21). Therefore, he is declaring by his statement that God is in Christ reconciling the world unto Himself (2 Corinthians 5:17–19).

Faith in its simplest definition is believing, trusting, depending, or relying on. By his next statement, we see the exercise of his faith. *"Lord, remember me when thou comest into thy kingdom."* Let that statement sink in for a moment. Now ask yourself this question: why would a dying man ask another dying Man to remember him when He comes to rule in His kingdom? Both would be dead in less than six hours!

Some would say that takes great faith. No. It takes a great Object of one's faith. It is not the amount of faith that matters; it is the object of that faith which determines the outcome. The thief came to understand that

- death was not the cessation of life;
- Jesus was God in the flesh;
- Jesus would literally die, be buried, and rise again;
- Jesus would be victorious over death, hell, and the grave;
- Jesus would come again and set up His kingdom;
- and he wanted to be part of that kingdom over which Jesus would rule.

Jesus saw his faith and assured him, *"To day shalt thou be with me in paradise."* God is not willing for any to perish. However, He demands repentance and faith in order to be saved from hell.

3.   Salvation Is by Grace through Faith

The last truth to be understood is grace. Grace is God's unmerited favor. It is God giving us what we do not deserve. No one deserves to go to heaven no matter how morally good or evil the individual is or has been. Grace is the most misunderstood part of a deathbed repentance. Many people, especially the unsaved, just won't believe that God can, should, or would allow someone, as we have previously described, to go to heaven at the eleventh hour.

The reason is they have a false concept of going to heaven. They believe that if their good deeds outweigh their bad deeds, then God will let them in. Therefore, since the person on the deathbed had no good deeds to speak of, that individual cannot go to heaven: that would be unfair to the rest of us who had tried to do right.

Nevertheless, no one has ever done enough good deeds to make it to heaven. The very best that even the pope can produce is filthy rags in the sight of God. *"But we are all as an unclean thing, and all our righteousnesses are as filthy rags"* (Isaiah 64:6).

If it were not for God's grace, no one could go.

> *For by grace are ye saved through faith; and that not of yourselves: it is the gift of God: Not of works, lest any man should boast.* (Ephesians 2:8–9)

> *Being justified freely by his grace through the redemption that is in Christ Jesus.* (Romans 3:24)

> *But where sin abounded, grace did much more abound.* (Romans 5:20)

> *For we know the grace of Our Lord Jesus Christ, that, though he was rich, yet for your sakes he became poor, that we through his poverty might be rich.* (2 Corinthians 8:9)

Even we who have exercised repentance toward God and faith in the Lord Jesus Christ are not sinless and perfect. We fall into sin after salvation and our faith falters along the way. The truth is we cannot produce enough good works after salvation to keep us saved. If it were not for *"the exceeding riches of his grace in his kindness towards us in Christ Jesus,"* we would not go to heaven either! The truth is we are saved by grace and we are kept saved by grace! (1 Peter 1:3–5)

Warren Wiersbe said, "The man was saved wholly by grace; it was the gift of God (Ephesians 2:8-9). He did not deserve it and he could not earn it. His salvation was personal and secure, guaranteed by the word of Jesus Christ. The man hoped for some kind of help in the future, but Jesus gave him forgiveness that very day, and he died and went with Jesus to paradise."

To deny all deathbed conversions is to deny the sufficiency of the death of Christ and make salvation the product of good works. This would also eliminate grace and give us bragging rights. And that stands in stark contradiction to what God said, "*Not of works, lest any man should boast.*"

The Price

What is the price for waiting to the last moment to be saved? I'll not go into great details at this time. However, there are rewards that believers can earn after they are saved. These rewards and crowns are thought to be laid at the feet of Jesus as a token of our love, devotion, and appreciation for His saving grace. This thief and others like him will have absolutely nothing to lie at the feet of Jesus when they get to heaven.

The Huge Warning

Although this account of the repentant thief is true, the Bible warns against waiting until the last minute. James 4:14 reminds us that our life is as a vapor that appears for a little while and then vanishes away. This speaks of the brevity of life. Hebrews 9:27 stresses that we have an appointment with death but it gives no indication as to when we will die, whether young or old. Second Corinthians 6:2 tells us that "*now is the accepted time; behold, now is the day of salvation.*" This serves as a warning that tomorrow could be too late.

Previously, I said that to deny all deathbed conversions is to deny the sufficiency of the death of Christ. It would be foolish to say all deathbed conversions are genuine. It would be judgmental to say no deathbed conversion is genuine. Nonetheless, we must exercise caution. The reason being, two men were crucified with Christ. Both men equally had access to the Saviour and made their petitions known to Him.

The first thief desired to be *saved from* the situation and the circumstances in which he found himself. His thoughts were for the here and now. On the other hand, the second thief accepted his guilt and its consequences. His desire was to *be saved to* spend eternity with Jesus Christ.

My friend, a person can sin away their day of grace as the first thief did. God can refuse to answer you in your time of greatest need. Take heed to these words found in Proverbs 1:23–31.

> *Turn you at my reproof: behold, I will pour out my spirit unto you, I will make known my words unto you. Because I have called, and ye have refused; I have stretched out my hand, and no man regarded; But ye have set at nought all my counsel, and would none of my reproof:*
>
> *I also will laugh at your calamity; I will mock when your fear cometh; When your fear cometh as desolation, and your destruction cometh as a whirlwind; when distress and anguish cometh upon you.*
>
> *Then shall they call upon me, but I will not answer, they shall seek me early, but they shall not find me: For that they hated knowledge, and did not choose the fear of the Lord: They would none of my counsel: they despised all my reproof.*
>
> *Therefore shall they eat the fruit of their own way, and be filled with their own devices.*

Listen carefully to Matthew Henry: "It is certain that true repentance is never too late, but it is as certain that late repentance is seldom true. It is a single instance in Scripture; it should teach us to despair of none, and that none should despair of themselves; but lest it should be abused, it is contrasted with the awful state of the other thief, who died hardened in unbelief, though a crucified Saviour was so near him. Be sure that in general men die as they live."

What about Marriage?

Will we still be considered married to our mates when we get to heaven? Jesus addresses this question in Matthew 22:23–33. In response to a hypothetical question, He reveals the arrangement of relationships between former husbands and wives. *"Jesus answered and said unto them, Ye do err, not knowing the scriptures, nor the power of God. For in the resurrection they neither marry, nor are given in marriage, but are as the angels of God in heaven"* (Matthew 22:29–30).

A friend of mine from New Mexico, Stan White, shared a wonderful tidbit with me and I haven't forgotten it. Stan was preaching at the funeral of a dear missionary friend. He spoke of his friend's love for God and how much he missed his wife since her death. Stan went on to say, "_____, upon his arrival in heaven, first wanted to see his Saviour's face and thank Him for His amazing grace. Once he has seen Jesus, the next person he wanted to see was his lovely wife who he missed so much." Stan went on to say, "I know the Lord said that we neither marry nor are given in marriage in heaven: but God didn't say we could not go steady. Amen!"

How Can There Be Darkness in Hell When Fire Is Present?

This question of darkness existing alongside of the fire to the human mind is an oxymoron. In the Word of God, we do find that hell, fire, and darkness coexist. It seems impossible to us. However, we must consider that all things are possible with God.

> But the children of the kingdom shall be cast
> out into outer darkness: there shall be weeping and
> gnashing of teeth. (Matthew 8:12)

And if thine eye offend thee, pluck it out, and cast it from thee: it is better for thee to enter into life with one eye, rather than having two eyes to be cast into hell fire. (Matthew 18:9)

For if God spared not the angels that sinned, but cast them down to hell, and delivered them into chains of darkness, to be reserved unto judgment. (2 Peter 2:4)

Adam Clarke's comment concerning the angels is interesting. "Chains of darkness; and so dense and strong is this darkness that it cannot be broken through; they cannot deliver themselves, nor be delivered by others."

Hell, fire, darkness: darkness so thick that it is inescapable yet flames which leap high but cannot light the way. Could this be symbolic language the scriptures are using? Well if it is, then the symbolism should be enough to turn anyone from a life of sin because the reality will be much worse than the symbol.

Another thing to consider is that the fires of hell are not like anything we are familiar with. The fires we have seen in this life not only produce light but also need combustible materials to exist. Nevertheless, this is not the case with the fires of hell. Jesus emphatically states three times in Mark 9:44, 46, and 48: *"Where the worm dieth not, and the fire is not quenched."*

This eternal flame never consumes its occupants either. How different is that from what we are used to? Evidence of such a statement can be proven from the Book of Revelation. Read the following verses of scripture very carefully.

And the beast was taken, and with him the false prophet that wrought miracles before him, with which he deceived them that had received the mark of the beast, and them that worshipped his image. These both were cast alive into a lake of fire burning with brimstone. (Revelation 19:20)

> *And when the thousand years are expired, Satan shall be loosed out of his prison, And shall go out to deceive the nations which are in the four quarters of the earth, Gog and Magog, to gather them together to battle: the number of whom is as the sand of the sea. And they went up on the breadth of the earth, and compassed the camp of the saints about, and the beloved city: and fire came down from God out of heaven, and devoured them. And the devil that deceived them was cast into the lake of fire and brimstone, where the beast and the false prophet are, and shall be tormented day and night for ever and ever.* (Revelation 20:7–10)

Did you see in Revelation 19:20 that two men were cast alive into the lake of fire burning with brimstone? However, when we come to Revelation 20:7, a thousand years have expired. Yet when we read verse 10 of the same chapter, Satan is cast into the lake of fire where the two men *are*! And the verse further reveals, they will exist unconsumed by the fire forever.

Eternal fire which never consumes its occupants, how strange is that? Nonetheless, there is one more thing we need to consider about hell, fire, and darkness.

Four times in Revelation the words "lake of fire" are used to describe the place in which the unsaved will be incarcerated forever. This is a fire unlike anything known to man. The implications suggest that it is in the form of a liquid, therefore implying that the occupants are totally engulfed as one is submerged when diving into a pool of water.

So how can darkness and fire coexist? First, because it is a fire unlike anything on earth. Second, because God said so and all things are possible with Him.

The Body after Death

Jack Wellman in his article "Donating One's Body to Science" said, "What can science learn from a dead body anyway? Probably many things, I am sure: but two things science will never allow us to do; to have a human, physical body last forever and to prevent one from dying. *I have seen the statistics on death and they are very impressive; one out of every one human die*" (italics mine).

Someone has said, and you have probably heard it before, that there are two things for certain in life: death and taxes. Sometimes death is expected because of some incurable disease. At other times, death completely takes us by surprise. In cases like this, many times the surviving loved ones are left with the burden of making the funeral arrangements.

Whether the burden falls unexpectedly upon the surviving family or whether the funeral is prearranged, in either case, the process is not always easy. Prearranged funerals do make it more bearable for the survivors.

Nevertheless, prearranged or not, there must be a decision as to what is going to happen to the body. The law of the land demands the proper disposal of the body after death. Common decency also expects no less of us.

However, what are my choices when it comes to disposing of my corpse or that of a loved one? There are at least four ways by which the body or corpse can be properly and legally taken care of.

1. green funeral or natural burial
2. cremation

3. donating one's body to science
4. tradition burial

The green or natural burial is not as common as the other three. The name green or natural implies the method by which the body is disposed of. In this method, the body is not embalmed and must be placed in a biodegradable coffin: pine wood, cardboard, wicker, or in a shroud. With this method, there are no headstones to mark the gravesite. Normally, a rock or stone is placed where the body is buried with the name, date of birth, and date of death written thereon.

Cremation has become a popular means of disposing of one's body after death. Sometimes, because of the financial burden, this is the method a person or family chooses to take care of their loved one. The process is self-explanatory. The body is placed in a cardboard box or coffin then carried and placed into the cremation chamber, also known as a retort. This chamber is heated to a temperature that ranges between 1400 to 1800 degrees Fahrenheit.

It takes between one to three hours to complete this process. Once the body has been completely burned, the remains are allowed to cool before the final process is made. Once the remains have cooled, they are placed into a cremulator where everything is reduced to a white powder weighing between three to seven pounds.

Donation to science is growing in popularity as well, and this is the least expensive option. There are no expenses for the family to bear and all means of transporting the loved one, after their death, is covered by the facility to which it is donated.

However, I have heard there are some prerequisites that must be met in order to be accepted. Arrangements must be made before the death of the individual, and they must have all their limbs intact. Once the research is over, the remains are normally cremated and returned to the family within a year at some facilities. Other than that, my knowledge is limited concerning this method.

Traditional burial is still the most common method used today. Yet with the rise in the popularity of cremation, it may soon outnumber traditional burials. Most people are more familiar with this method of care in the death of their loved one. The only difference between this and the natural or green burial is the body is embalmed, placed in a casket, and the casket into a vault.

These are the four methods with which I am acquainted with and are the legal means of properly taking care of our loved ones who have preceded us in death.

Occasionally, I am asked, what does the Bible say about cremation, donating one's body to science, or by their question inferring, is traditional burial the only option for believers?

So does the Bible address these concerns? Since the biggest difference between green or natural burial and traditional burial is embalming, these two will be addressed under traditional burial.

Cremation: What Does the Bible Say about It?

Dr. Harold Sightler was asked this question: Is it right to cremate the dead? His response: "It is a common practice, today, to burn the bodies of some who die. This practice is becoming more common. However, the Bible, as far as I can tell, is silent on this subject. Whether the body is burned or buried, it shall rise on resurrection morn. Personally, I do not approve of cremation."

In addition to Dr. Sightler's comment, I would like to say that whenever the Bible is silent on any subject of which we are concerned, there is no "thou shalt" or "thou shalt not." It is a wise individual who will search for a biblical illustration or principle that will aid them to make the right decision.

There are several accounts in the Bible where the bodies of the dead were burned, and one may use these accounts to help them in deciding to be or not to be cremated.

The first account is found in Joshua 6–7. You should read the account, but for the sake of time and space, I will summarize that account. The nation of Israel conquered and defeated the city of Jericho. Before the battle, Joshua had clearly commanded the people that absolutely no one was to be spared, except Rahab and her family. He also informed them that all silver, gold, vessels of iron and brass were to be consecrated unto the Lord (Joshua 6:17–19).

Achan, one of the Israelite soldiers, saw and decided to take for himself a Babylonian garment, two hundred shekels of silver, and a wedge of gold fifty shekels in weight. He hid them in the ground under his tent. Even though no one knew of his deed, God knew, and because of his disobedience to God's command, Israel suffered defeat and loss of life in their battle against Ai.

When his sin was discovered, Joshua asked, "*Why hast thou troubled us? The Lord shall trouble thee this day. And all Israel stoned him with stones, and burned them with fire. After they had stoned them with stones, they raised over him a great heap of stones unto this day. So the Lord turned from the fierceness of his anger*" (Joshua 7:25–26).

The second account is recorded in 1 Samuel 31:8–13. The first king of Israel, Saul, and his three sons were killed during a battle with the Philistines. When their bodies were discovered by the enemy, they cut off their heads and fastened their bodies to the wall of the city Beth-shan as a public display of victory.

In response to this, the valiant men of Jabesh-gilead went into action: "*And when the inhabitants of Jabesh-gilead heard of that which the Philistines had done to Saul; All the valiant men arose, and went all night, and took the body of Saul and the bodies of his sons from the wall of Beth-shan, and came to Jabesh, and burned them there. And they took their bones, and buried them under a tree at Jabesh, and fasted seven days*" (1 Samuel 31:11–13).

The third and fourth accounts are found in the book of Amos: The first in Amos 2:1 and the second in Amos 6:8–10. In the first account, God is about to judge the Moabites because of their transgressions. What was their transgression? "*Thus saith the LORD; For three transgressions of Moab, and for four, I will not turn away the punishment thereof; because he burned the bones of the king of Edom into lime.*"

Listen to Warren Wiersbe's comments: "What was the sin of Moab? Disrespect for the dead and for royalty. We don't know which king's remains were subjected to this humiliation, but the deed disgraced the memory of the king and humiliated the people of Edom."

And God was angry!

The last passage is Amos 6:8–10. God is about to judge the nation of Israel because they have sinned against Him. He is going to use the Assyrians as His instrument of judgment. He reveals that entire families would die.

With such a massive amount of dead bodies, burial would be such a slow process; disease from decaying bodies would rapidly spread to the survivors. Therefore, the dead would be burned by the surviving family members.

"And it shall come to pass, if there remain ten men in one house, that they shall die. And a man's uncle shall take him up, and he that burneth them, to bring out the bones of the house, and say unto him that is by the sides of the house, Is there any yet with thee? And he shall say, No."

Dr. Sightler is right. The Bible does not in any way say that cremation is a sin. It is silent on the matter. However, it does give some accounts where cremation was practiced. The wise individual will examine these accounts and determine whether it is a wise decision to be cremated or not. Let's revisit for a moment.

Of the four cases presented, one provoked God to judgment. That was the case of Amos 2:1, where the king of Moab showed dishonor and disrespect toward a king who had died and was already buried.

In the other three cases—Achan in Joshua 7, Saul and his sons in 1 Samuel 31, and the massive death in Amos 6—each of these could be seen as a matter of purification. The burning of Achan and his family was Israel's way of purifying the nation from Achan's sin of disobedience and covetousness. The cremation of Saul and his sons would symbolize cleansing from the defilement and disrespect done to them by the Philistines. Finally, the judgment of God judgment upon Israel would result in massive death. This would be an appropriate measure to prevent further death by the spread of disease.

We must also take this into account when considering God's point of view on this subject. Though God has not given a direct command against cremation, consider the occasions and the reasons for the action.

Cremation was the exception to the rule, not the normal means by which the dead were disposed of. In each case, cremation is associated with judgment or purification. How? In the Word of God, fire is the means by which God either judges or purifies.

In 1 Corinthians 3:11–15, the believer's works will be tried by fire at the Judgment Seat of Christ. This fire will reveal and remove all things that Christians have not done for the glory of God. Only that which is left after passing through the fire, if anything, will necessitate a reward.

Sodom and Gomorrah were destroyed by fire. God saw their wickedness and judged them swiftly (Genesis 19).

Second Peter 3:4–13 reminds us that this world has an appointment with fire. That the elements are going to melt with fervent heat, all the works will be burned with fire, and all these things shall be dissolved. Therefore, it is safe to say that man will not destroy this earth because God has reserved it *"unto fire against the day of judgment and perdition of ungodly men."*

However, if one's consideration or inclination toward cremation is to escape the judgment of God, perish the thought. The destruction of the body cannot destroy the soul. *"And fear not them which kill the body, but are not able to kill the soul: but rather fear him which is able to destroy both soul and body in hell"* (Matthew 10:28).

Many have died or were buried at sea. Their bodies have decomposed into millions of pieces: what was not eaten by fish. Nevertheless, God will put their decomposed, consumed, and reconsumed bodies back together again. They and all who have died no matter how the body was disposed of will have their day in God's courtroom. *"And the sea gave up the dead which were in it, and death and hell delivered up the dead which were in them: and they were judged every man according to their works"* (Revelation 20:13).

Even though there is only one case in which God's disapproval is clearly seen, cremation and its association with purification and judgment should aid you and me in our decision about cremation. It is a matter of personal choice. Whatever one's choice may be, cremation is the destruction or disposal of the body, but always remember the soul of man is eternal and will spend eternity in heaven or hell!

Donation to Science: What Does the Bible Say about It?

The popularity of donating one's body to science is also on the rise. This could be due to the high cost of a traditional funeral or the genuine concern for helping the advancements in the medical field.

Unlike cremation, where there are some examples or illustrations given for the individual to consider, I know of absolutely nothing in the Bible that remotely addresses this matter. Embalming is mentioned in Genesis 50:2, 26. Physicians are mentioned in verse 2 as well. As a matter of fact, donating one's organs to another individual is also mentioned, but more on that later.

Though the Bible is silent on the matter, people are not. Opinions can be presented on both sides of the issue: from the side of medical research, an individual would argue for the advancement of medical treatments learned from their gift to science. Others would argue for the quality of life that such a gift could offer, especially if someone is diagnosed with the same disease they had. These and other arguments are fair. If they are truly for the benefit of others, then I believe they are legitimate.

On the other side of the coin, some would argue this point: the body is the temple of God, and it is. They would remind us of 1 Corinthians 6:19–20 where the Apostle Paul says, "*What? Know ye not that your body is the temple of the Holy Ghost which is in you, which ye have of God, and ye are not your own? For ye are bought with a price: therefore glorify God in your body and in your spirit, which are God's.*"

No born-again believer would attempt to argue with that passage of scripture. Nevertheless, when the body dies, it becomes an empty shell. And if burial is the mode of disposing of the body, then the body will return to the dust from which it came (Ecclesiastes 12:7; Genesis 3:19).

Others would disagree by defending the Bible's prohibition against self-mutilation. The passage used for this prohibition is Leviticus 19:28: "*Ye shall not make any cuttings in your flesh for the dead, nor print any marks upon you: I am the Lord.*" However, this command is clearly given to those who are alive, not for those who have died.

However, we should also consider Deuteronomy 34:5–6. This is the biblical account of the death and burial of Moses. "*So Moses the servant of the Lord died there in the land of Moab, according to the word of the Lord. And he* [God] *buried him* [Moses] *in a valley in the land of Moab, over against Beth-peor: but no man knoweth of his sepulchre unto this day.*"

Yes, you read it correctly. God Himself buried Moses's body and he is the only character in all of history of whom this is said. In light of this, is this a prohibition against donating one's body to science for research?

Personally, I believe God is silent on the subject, and therefore, this matter again becomes a matter of personal preference.

However, if you are considering donating your body to science, what are your motives? Is it merely a cheap means of disposing of the corpse or are you genuinely concerned about the advancement of medical research and improving the quality of life for survivors?

John Piper made two interesting points on this subject. One, are there any small children involved? How would this affect them when there would be no body of a mom or dad or even a grave to visit during the healing process?

Second, one could even consider the analogy of Christ's body. Surely the human body that Christ took on was not designed to be tortured, whipped, lacerated, speared, and nailed to the cross like a piece of meat. But all those indignities were embraced by Christ: He chose them and He submitted to them. Not only that, our souls might be saved but precisely so that our bodies would be raised from the dead.

Reverently, I say this: Christ donated Himself freely for the payment of our sins. He freely gave Himself totally, without any reservation, to pay a debt He did not owe. No one could give themselves to science or for any other reason to accomplish what He has accomplished. And there is nothing that we could give Him in return, except our heart. Before you give your body to science, have you given your heart to Jesus?

If not, that is more important than all the medical field could ever learn from your dead body.

Burial: What Does the Bible Say about It?

This is the most common method of taking care of a loved one's body after death found in the Bible. There are well over two hundred total references to *bury, burial, burying, buried, grave,* and *tomb* in the Bible.

The first mention of the word *buried* is found in Genesis 15:15, where God told Abraham that he would be *"buried in a good old age."* In like manner, the first mention of the word *bury* is found in Genesis 23:4 where Abraham sought permission to purchase a piece of property "that I might bury my dead [Sarah, his wife] out of my sight."

Yet by what means the dead were disposed of before then, the Bible does not say. We know from scripture that Abel was the first human being to die at the hands of his brother Cain. What Cain did with the body of Abel, we cannot dogmatically say. The only thing we can say for sure is what God said to Cain: *"the voice of thy brother's blood crieth unto me from the ground"* (Genesis 4:8–10).

Did Cain bury the body? Did Cain dump Abel's body into a ravine? Surely Cain did something to hide or dispose of Abel's body, but just what, we can't say. However, one thing is for sure: God did not condemn Cain for how he disposed of Abel's body; He condemned him for shedding Abel's blood.

Once we leave the scene of the first murder in human history, there are approximately two thousand years before God mentions the burial of Abraham. Hundreds of thousands have died since Abel. As a matter of fact, the entire population of the earth, except for eight people, died in the flood. What happened to those corpses? It was impossible for Noah to have buried them. Their bodies would have decomposed and rotted by the time Noah left the ark. It is not impossible that God buried them, but it is highly improbable that He did.

In the New Testament account of Lazarus and the rich man (Luke 16:19–31), the rich man was buried but Lazarus was not. Since he was poor, it is very probable that he was cast into the Valley of Hinnom or Gehenna. This was the landfill of our day, located just outside the city of Jerusalem. The trash and refuse were disposed of there and the fires never went out. It was also the place where the unloved or unwanted dead were thrown to be burned. Jesus often used this place to illustrate that awful place called hell because, like Gehenna, the fires of hell will burn for eternity.

Jesus, before His incarnation, existed in Spirit form as did the Father. In Hebrews 10:5, Jesus said, "*Sacrifices and offerings thou wouldest not, but a body thou hast prepared me.*" I think this is an important concept we need to ponder. Why a body? The reason being a spirit is invisible and Jesus came to reveal the Father to fallen humanity. How?

First, the body would be the means of personal communication and tangible proof for the existence of God. The Apostle John in 1 John 1:1–4, rejoiced to convey these truths about the Lord Jesus: "*We have heard… we have seen… we have looked upon… our hands have handled… our fellowship is… with the Son.*"

Then in the Gospel of John 14:9, Jesus emphatically declared, "*He that hath seen me hath seen the Father.*"

Second, the body would be the means by which sin's debt would be paid in full. The wages of sin demanded death. Even though Jesus had many pre-incarnate appearances before Bethlehem, none of them could have been offered as a sacrifice for sin. He had to be made like unto His brethren; therefore, He assumed a physical body in the womb of Mary. As a Spirit, He did not die. However, as a man, His body was offered, His blood was shed, and as a man, He died on the cross.

Third, the body is the means by which He will have His eternal existence after the resurrection. Ever since resurrection day, Christ Jesus has had a body in which He will dwell for eternity. "*For there is one God, and one mediator between God and men, the man Christ Jesus; Who gave himself a ransom for all, to be testified in due time*" (1 Timothy 2:5–6).

Fourth, His bodily resurrection guarantees the resurrection of our body. Jesus was placed in the tomb with a physical body just like ours. Yet when He came out of the tomb, He did not come out a Spirit; He came out with a glorified body. He told His disciples on resurrection day, *"Behold my hands and my feet, that it is I myself: handle me, and see; for a spirit hath not flesh and bones, as ye see me have"* (Luke 24:39).

The Apostle Paul speaks of the resurrected body in 1 Corinthians 15:35–50. He reveals the truth that our body will be sown a natural body but raised a spiritual or glorified body like unto Christ's glorious body (Philippians 3:20–21).

One must remember that the body is just a temporary dwelling place for the soul. It is not to be worshipped, nor is it to be disrespected after our death. Great care is demonstrated throughout scripture when it came to the death of a loved one. Even in the death of the Lord Jesus, Joseph and Nicodemus took time to prepare the body of Christ for burial (John 19:38–42).

In like manner, on Sunday, very early in the morning, came others with spices to anoint the body of Jesus (Luke 23:55–24:1) This care and respect for the dead can never be exhibited when a body is cremated or donated to science.

But to say that burial is the only acceptable option to God for disposing of a loved one's corpse I think would be overstepping the bounds of Scripture. But to say, I prefer burial over other options because that is the method my Lord and Saviour used is quite another. And personally, I do prefer burial over all the rest.

Whatever method one may choose—donating to science, cremation, or burial—the fact remains there is a Judgment Day with God. The method of disposing of the body will not prevent one's day in God's courtroom. The resurrection will see to it.

One last thing before we leave this chapter.

Organ Donation: What Does the Bible Say about It?

Earlier, I said the Bible speaks about organ donation. This is another subject upon which many disagree for whatever reason. Some of the arguments against donation to science and even cremation could be used to say it is wrong to donate any of our organs while living or upon death, even though it would help improve the quality of life for someone else.

I know of only one passage of scripture that addresses this issue. It is found in Galatians 4:15: "*Where is then the blessedness ye spoke of? For I bear you record, that, if it had been possible, ye would have plucked out your own eyes, and have given them to me.*"

It is very possible, according to the passage of Scripture, that Paul had trouble with his eyes. The people of Galatia knew it, and according to Paul's own testimony, he said they would have gladly given to him their eyes, *if it were possible*, to improve his quality of life.

This is my opinion: if organ donation had been possible in his day, and it was a sin, Paul would have rebuked them for it. Nevertheless, he didn't; therefore, this is also a matter of personal preference.

Near-Death Experiences

There have been numerous occasions through the years, of individuals, who have had near-death or out-of-the-body experiences. Books and movies have resulted from such occasions. For instance, *90 Minutes in Heaven* by Don Piper, *Divine Revelation of Hell* by Mary K. Baxter, and the book followed by the movie *Heaven is for Real.*

On two separate occasions, people I personally know related their experiences to me. The first gentlemen said his occurred while on the operating table and upon his recovery. He told what he saw and heard while the surgeons attended to him.

The other told me his encounter with death, if I remember correctly, happened while hunting. He had a heart attack, died, and was brought back to life. What he experienced was the most beautiful place he had ever seen, a peaceful place and that he was not afraid to die now.

Countless others have experienced the same or similar encounters. But how credible are these experiences? Should we put any stock in them? Or are they the results of a vivid imagination? However, more importantly, what does the Bible have to say about it, if anything?

First, the Bible has a lot to say about people who were raised from the dead.

1. Elijah, in 1 Kings 17, raised the son of the widow who lived in Zarephath from the dead.
2. Elisha, in 2 Kings 4, in like manner, raised the son of the Shunammite woman from the dead.

3. Even after Elisha died, he was responsible for the resurrection of a man from the dead. The account is found in 2 Kings 13:20–21.

4. Jesus in the New Testament raised several from the dead, with Lazarus being most familiar (John 11:1-44).

5. Peter, in Acts 9:36–43, raised Dorcas from the dead.

6. Paul, in Acts 20:6–12, raised a young man by the name Eutychus from the dead after he had fallen from a window at midnight.

7. In Matthew 27:51–53, we read of the account concerning the death of Christ. When Jesus died on the cross, several miraculous things took place at that moment. One of those miracles is as follows: "*And the graves were opened; and many bodies of the saints which slept* [died] *arose, And came out of the graves after his resurrection, and went into the holy city, and appeared unto many.*"

In each and every case presented, these individuals were dead—graveyard dead. Not any of these cases would qualify for a near-death or out-of-the-body experience. The soul had departed their bodies, they had entered into their eternal realm, were brought back to physical life, and unfortunately, though, they died again.

There is one important thing I would like for you to see concerning those who were raised from the dead. You will never read in the Bible where any of these people told their family or friends where they went, what they did, what they heard, or what they saw.

Surely if one of them had entered the regions of the damned, he would have warned his family and friends of this awful place. Equally so, if one had entered into the regions of the blessed, he or she would not have been silent about it.

The Bible is silent as to the number of people who came out of the graves when Jesus arose from the dead. However, it says, "*Many... saints came out of the graves... and went... and appeared unto many.*" This is no isolated case. This is not one here and there but an occasion upon which multiple people were seen at the same time. Their death and now their appearance was witnessed by many. Surely if someone had said anything about where they had been, revival would have broken out in Jerusalem! But mum is the word of the day.

None of these examples qualifies for near-death or out-of-the-body experiences. Nevertheless, their silence on the matter speaks volumes.

Second, there are only two examples given in scriptures which might be considered out-of-the-body experiences: 2 Corinthians 12:1–5 and Revelation 4:1–4. To my knowledge, there are no near-death experiences recorded.

Second Corinthians 12:2–4 reads, "*I knew a man in Christ above fourteen years ago, (whether in the body, I cannot tell; or out of the body, I cannot tell: God knoweth;) such a one caught up to the third heaven. And I knew such a man, (whether in the body, or out of the body, I cannot tell: God knoweth;) How that he was caught up into paradise, and heard unspeakable words, which it is not lawful for a man to utter.*"

According to the text, this individual, most of whom, I also, believe is the Apostle Paul, was not sure of the mode of transportation, but he was sure of his final destination.

Now, we cannot be dogmatic as to the situation Paul is referring to. He does not name the event nor the place where this occurred. Nevertheless, some have tried to fit this account into the time when Paul was stoned at Lystra. They do so by subtracting the "*above fourteen years ago*" from the date he wrote to the church in Corinth.

This account is recorded in Acts 14:1–20. The hostility which leads to the stoning of the Apostle Paul began in the city of Iconium. Paul and his partner Barnabas left Iconium and headed for Derbe and Lystra to escape being stoned to death. While at Lystra, the unbelieving Jews from Iconium came and persuaded the people of Lystra to stone him. And when they were finished, they "*drew him out of the city, supposing he had been dead. Howbeit, as the disciples stood round about him, he rose up, and came into the city*" (Acts 14:19–20).

Could this be the account Paul is referring to and the time when he was actually "caught up into paradise"? If it is, then, we could say he had an out-of-the-body experience. However, Paul wasn't sure whether he was in the body or out of the body. Paul was certain of one thing—he had entered the "third heaven" which is the abode of God.

But Acts 14, honestly does not seem to fit the time or the place of Paul's experience in 2 Corinthians 12. One obvious reason being, the disciples who *"stood round about him"* as he lay outside the city. They would have known if his body left the earth and returned.

It seems possible that Paul's experience took place somewhere other than Lystra. It is my personal opinion, since Paul was not sure, *"whether in the body, or out of the body, I cannot tell: God knoweth,"* that Paul's experience took place when he was by himself. Nevertheless, when, where, and how this took place, the Apostle Paul definitely left the earthly realm, entered into "Paradise," and returned. This cannot be denied!

Does Paul's situation qualify for either a near-death or out-of-the-body experience? We can't say dogmatically either way because Paul himself was not sure.

However, there are a couple of thoughts I'd like to share concerning Paul's experience.

1. Paul, unlike those of our day, kept quiet about his experience for more than fourteen years.
2. Paul was not given permission by God to talk about the things he experienced. He said, *"He was caught up into paradise and heard unspeakable words, which it is not lawful for a man to utter."*

Warren Wiersbe said, "He overheard the divine secrets that are shared only in heaven. These things could be spoken by God and by beings in heaven, but they could not be spoken by men."

Revelation 4:1-2 reads, *"After this I looked, and, behold, a door was opened in heaven: and the first voice which I heard was as it were a trumpet talking with me; which said, Come up hither, and I will shew thee things which must be hereafter. And immediately I was in the spirit: and, behold, a throne was set in heaven, and one sat on the throne."*

The Apostle John at this point was exiled to the isle of Patmos because of his stand for Jesus Christ (Revelation 1:9). While there, God unveiled to His servant future events that will happen in the last days. According to chapter 4, John is caught up into heaven where he sees the throne and He who sat on that throne: God. He sees twenty-four seats, four beasts full of eyes, a scroll in the right hand of Him who sat on the throne, the Lamb which is Christ Jesus, and he hears a song of praise to the Lamb Who is worthy of all glory.

We don't know how long John and Paul were caught up in heaven. But we know this: God permitted one to write some of what he heard and saw while restricting the other one altogether.

John MacArthur in his article "Are Visits to Heaven for Real" says, "We live in a narcissistic culture, and it shows in these accounts of people who claim they've been to heaven. They... *keeping themselves in the foreground... say comparatively little about God or His glory.* Instead, (they're) obsessed with details like how they felt—how peaceful, how happy, how comfortable they were, how... enlightening their experience was... *they highlight everything but what's truly important about heaven.* But if you actually saw heaven and lived to tell about it, those things are not what would capture your heart and imagination. *You would be preoccupied instead with the majesty and grace of the One whose glory fills the place*" (italics mine).

Notice how the Apostle John responded when he saw the Lord Jesus in Revelation 1:17. What were the elders and the beasts doing when John entered the throne room of God in Revelation 4–5? Who were they preoccupied with: themselves or God and His Son? Not themselves!

Neither of the examples given fit the near-death experience. Only John's account in the book of Revelation would come close to an out-of-the-body experience.

This is not to say others in the Bible never had a vision of heaven. Isaiah had such a vision in Isaiah 6:1–8. Ezekiel had visions of God in Ezekiel 1:1. Micaiah also saw the Lord sitting on His throne in 2 Chronicles 18:18. Stephen saw the Lord standing on the right hand of God in Acts 7:54–60.

That being said, one needs to be extremely careful when it comes to near-death or out-of-the-body experiences whether our own or someone else's. This caution is fourfold:

1. How does this experience compare with what the Bible says about it? Does this experience exceed what the Bible clearly reveals? If so, then you have what is known as extra-biblical revelation. This is clearly not of God, and one must remember, Satan is always ready to deceive anyone he can.

   In the words of John MacArthur, "We need to accept the boundaries God Himself has put on what He has revealed. It is sheer folly to speculate where the Scripture is silent. And it is seriously dangerous to listen to anyone who claims to know more about God, heaven, angels or the afterlife than God Himself has revealed to us in Scripture."

2. The "light" which is usually mentioned in all encounters of near-death experiences: what is that light? Why do most people say they followed it? Is it because "light" is associated with good and "darkness" with evil?

   Again, extreme caution must be exercised. Second Corinthians 11:13–15 reminds us that Satan is capable of transforming himself *"into an angel of light."* This is why it is so important to know what you believe, why you believe it, and more importantly, be able to prove it biblically.

3. It is not impossible, for all things are possible with God, but it is highly improbable, that God will grant such an experience in this day and time. Since the completion of the Bible, visions, along with the experiences of Paul and John, are not needed. All we'll ever need to know about heaven, hell, and the afterlife are found in the Bible.

   But, and if one is allowed to experience this and it is of God, it should never be used or told as a tool to witness to others. The scriptural basis for this can be seen in the account of Lazarus and the rich man in Luke 15:19–31.

The rich man died, and in hell, he lifted up his eyes being in torments. Upon his arrival, he made a couple of requests. The last request was that Abraham would send Lazarus back from the dead to tell his five brothers of this awful place. Abraham refused, and his words were these: "*They have Moses and the prophets; let them hear them. And he said, Nay, father Abraham: but if one went to them from the dead, they will repent. And he said unto him, If they hear not Moses and the prophets, neither will they be persuaded though one rose from the dead.*"

What is Abraham saying? The Word of God, not experiences, is the only acceptable means by which salvation can come.

4. Where experience in such cases contradict the Word of God or add to the Word of God: the Word must be accepted over the experience. There is no other option for the Christian and nothing more damning for the unbeliever.

John MacArthur said, "Those who demand to know more than Scriptures tell us about heaven are sinning."

> "*The secret things belong unto the Lord our God: but those things which are revealed belong to us and to our children for ever, that we may do all the words of this law*" (Deuteronomy 29:29).

The limits of our curiosity are established by the boundary of biblical revelation even though many of our questions may go unanswered!

In conclusion, if such an experience would come and be allowed by God, it will coincide with what is already revealed in the Word of God and ultimately bring honor and glory to the Lord Jesus Christ.

The essential thing for all believers to do is found in Acts 17:11: "*They received the word with readiness of mind, and searched the scriptures daily, whether those things were so.*"

Dealing with Grief

Grief is a natural response when a loved one dies. It is an emotion that's just as real as love, joy, peace, and anger. Nevertheless, how one grieves and expresses that grief rest entirely on one's personality.

Even members of the same family will express their grief in different ways. One may be loud and uncontrollable, while another may suppress it until they are alone.

However one expresses their grief, it is a natural part of the healing process. And the time frame of healing will also differ according to the individual.

As a pastor, I have witnessed the death of many of God's people. I have seen those who have wept uncontrollably, while others with tear-filled eyes whispered, "I love you. See you later."

Why do family members respond so differently? First of all, their personalities are different. Secondly, their understanding of the Bible may vary. One could be focusing on the immediate situation and the pain they are experiencing while the other is focusing on eternity.

Does this mean that one displays a greater love than the other? Of course not. It only reveals the perspective from which they're viewing death. And that source will determine the degree of grief they will experience. It will also decide the time frame of the healing process.

Does the Bible say anything about grief? Yes! It gives us example after example of those who experienced grief. For instance, Job lost his entire family and finances all in one day. Naomi lost her husband and two sons while in a foreign country. King David's son died just a few days after birth. All of them responded differently to their loss as you can see.

Job: "*The Lord gave, and the Lord hath taken away; blessed be the name of the Lord*" (Job 1:21).

Naomi: "*For the Almighty hath dealt bitterly with me. I went out full, and the Lord hath brought me home again empty*" (Ruth 1:20–21).

David: "*But now he is dead, wherefore should I fast? Can I bring him back again?*" (2 Samuel 12:23).

In the John 11:35, the most profound statement ever made is "*Jesus wept.*" How immeasurable those words are! How humane our Creator is that He would weep when one of His creatures dies! How comforting this is to those who are experiencing the loss of a loved one.

Imagine God Who is holy and righteous taking upon Himself flesh and blood. Why? To become one of us so that He might experience the same pain, heartache, and trials we do, ensuring that He is able to sympathize with us in our weaknesses (Hebrews 2:9–18, 4:14–16).

Thus, an understanding of why God became one of us will enrich one's perspective of death. It will not eliminate the grief. It will, however, bring you comfort knowing that God understands what you are facing and that you're not facing it alone.

How Does One Start the Healing Process?

Healing, whether physical or emotional, must be treated properly in order for restoration to be possible. Any view of death, any ideology concerning the afterlife, and any effort to console the heart without the Word of God is futile.

Alcohol, drugs (legal or illegal), a psychiatrist or psychologist can help mask the pain temporarily. However, this may carry a hefty price tag, both physically and financially.

The Bible is the only reliable medicine that brings relief and healing to the brokenhearted. God is the Great Physician, and His services come at no cost to you. They were paid in full by the Lord Jesus Christ when He died on Calvary. The Psalmist declares, "*He healeth the broken in heart, and bindeth up their wounds*" (Psalm 147:3).

I don't profess to have all the answers to what you are experiencing. However, God, through His Word, can comfort everyone who is struggling with grief. He is the "*God of all comfort; Who comforteth us in all our tribulation, that we may be able to comfort them which are in any trouble, by the comfort wherewith we ourselves are comforted of God*" (2 Corinthians 1:3–4).

God desires for you to be emotionally healthy. And He is willing and able to restore your emotional well-being. Through your restoration, He can use you to help those in similar situations.

The Healing Process:

• First, Realize That Grieving Is Not a Sin; It's Natural

Throughout the Bible, we find multiple examples of individuals grieving over the death of loved ones. Abraham mourned and wept when Sarah died (Genesis 23:2). Joseph and his brothers mourned the death of their father Jacob for seventy days (Genesis 50:1–3). Mary, Martha, and Jesus wept at the grave of Lazarus (John 11:1–37).

Grief is the emotional sorrow exhibited by one who has lost anything or anyone they were deeply attached to. It is the natural response and God-given ability to relieve unbearable pain. It is needful, it is expected, and it is understood by God.

However, grief can become sinful when one refuses to accept God's teaching concerning death. First Thessalonians 4:13 reads, "*But I would not have you to be ignorant, brethren, concerning them which are asleep, that ye sorrow not, even as others which have no hope.*" Ignorance is one thing but a willful rejection of God's Word is sinful. It is the truth which can set you free from unwarranted grief (John 8:32).

Grief is also sinful when one abuses their body. Leviticus 19:28 reads, "*Ye shall not make any cuttings in your flesh for the dead, nor print any marks upon you: I am the LORD.*" Uncontrollable grief can and has resulted in the abuse of one's body. Cutting oneself, beating oneself, and or attempting suicide because of grief is sinful.

Grief becomes sin when one is blaming God for their circumstances. Whenever a loved one, whether a parent, mate, and especially a child dies, it can have adverse effects on the survivors. Instead of grief driving one into the arms of a loving God, grief drives a wedge and they begin to blame God.

They know all things are possible with God and that He could have prevented their loved one's death. Since He didn't, He is responsible for their grief.

Grief can also cloud the mind to the truth of God. God is Omniscient, Omnipresent, and Omnipotent. He never does anything off the cuff. There is always a purpose, a plan, and His glory involved in all He does or allows.

June Hunt said, "God does not find pleasure in bringing grief to His beloved children, but He does what He does from His position as the sovereign, all-knowing, all-loving God."

Lamentations 3:32–33 reads, "*But though he caused grief, yet he will have compassion according to the multitude of his mercies. For he doth not afflict willingly nor grieve the children of men.*"

- Second, Grief Is Meant to Be Temporary

Nowhere in scripture are we forbidden to weep or grief for the dead; however, excessive grief is. "*Weeping may endure for a night, but joy cometh in the morning*" (Psalm 30:5).

While God puts no time frame on grief, excessive or prolonged grief could indicate a lack of understanding concerning those who have preceded us in death.

> But I would not have you to be ignorant, brethren, concerning them which are asleep [have died], that ye sorrow not, even as others which have no hope. For if we believe that Jesus died and rose again, even so them which also sleep in Jesus will God bring with him.
>
> For this we say unto you by the word of the Lord, that we which are alive and remain unto the coming of the Lord shall not prevent them which are asleep. For the Lord himself shall descend from heaven with a shout, with the voice of the archan-

*gel, and with the trump of God: and the dead in
Christ shall rise first:*

*Then we which are alive and remain shall be
caught up together with them in the clouds, to meet
the Lord in the air: and so shall we ever be with
the Lord. Wherefore comfort one another with these
words.* (1 Thessalonians 4:13–18)

The Lord is drawing a distinction in this passage between the Christian and the non-Christian. The non-Christian may have no understanding concerning the departed dead. To some, the dead are dead; there is no afterlife. Therefore, little to no grief is expressed. To others, grief consumes their very life.

To the survivor, their whole world just collapsed. The departed were the heart, soul, and reason for life itself. And now they're gone. How will they survive without the love of his or her life?

Then others grieve because they do not understand what happens to those who die. Their grief stems from unanswered questions like where are they, what are they doing, are they happy, and will I ever see them again?

The Christian is not exempt from grief either. He or she may have many questions, but they find that God provides the answers to these questions in His Word. And these answers help lighten the load.

We know God sees our grief and does not condemn us for it. God takes notice of every tear we cry. Listen to Psalms 56:8: "*Thou tellest my wanderings: put thou my tears into thy bottle: are they not in thy book?*" How much comfort this verse brings to the heart of the believer.

Tears are liquid words. They express what the heart and mind cannot fathom. However, God knows and records the story each teardrop tells in His book. What an awesome God we have!

Charles Spurgeon said, "We may sorrow, but with measure and limit. We know that the souls of the departed are safe, that their bodies will rise from the grave. Wherefore, then, should we weep and lament as the heathen and unbelieving?"

The knowledge of the state of the believer, absent from the body and present with the Lord (2 Corinthians 5:1–8), the assurance of Christ returning with the departed saints as seen in 1 Thessalonians 4:13–18, the guarantee of the resurrection (1 Corinthians 15:1–57), and our reunion with those who have gone before us—these truths are given by God to lift you out of your grief.

- Third, Grief Needs to Be Expressed

Grief can have physical, emotional, or spiritual ramifications when one bottles it up inside. Crying is God's relief valve when the pressures of life become more than we can bear.

Listen to how grief affected David before he called out to God: *"Have mercy upon me, O LORD, for I am in trouble: mine eye is consumed with grief, yea, my soul and my belly. For my life is spent with grief and my years with sighing: my strength faileth me because of mine iniquity, and my bones are consumed"* (Psalm 31:9–10).

Nevertheless, sharing one's grief with others is another way to relieve a burdened heart. But with whom?

The Psalmist often shared his burdens with the Lord, and who better to share our grief with than Him? Listen to Psalm 61:1–4: *"Hear my cry, O God; attend unto my prayer. From the end of the earth will I cry unto thee, when my heart is overwhelmed: lead me to the rock that is higher than I. For thou hast been a shelter for me, and a strong tower from the enemy. I will abide in thy tabernacle for ever: I will trust in the covert of thy wings."*

It is interesting to notice as one reads through the Psalms that the psalmist never ends up where he begins. He may start out between a rock and a hard place, but almost without fail, he will be standing upon the rock praising God. Such is the case in this and the previous Psalms we read.

In Psalm 31, he ends with verse 24: *"Be of good courage, and he shall strengthen your heart, all ye that hope in the Lord."* Then he finishes Psalm 61 with verse 8: *"So will I sing praise unto thy name for ever, that I may daily perform my vows."*

When we commune with God—expressing our grief, our concerns, even our fears—and we are open to His Word and love, then like the psalmist, we will leave differently than we arrived.

In like manner, the church family is designed to help ease the burdens of one another. Galatians 6:2 says, *"Bear ye one another's burdens, and so fulfill the law of Christ."* Romans 12:15 instructs us, *"Rejoice with them that do rejoice, and weep with them that weep."* First Corinthians 12:12–26 speaks of the unity and union of the church body. Our union to one another is such that when one member suffers or rejoices, the remaining members join in.

God has established a relief system for grief. If one fails to use God's provisions, then grief management becomes difficult. But in Christ, we find strength and courage to carry on.

He invites us to come to Him: *"Come unto me, all ye that labour and are heavy laden, and I will give you rest"* (Matthew 11:28). And He encourages us to leave our burdens with Him because He cares for us. *"Casting all your care upon him; for he careth for you"* (1 Peter 5:7).

- Fourth, Overcoming Grief Is Illustrated

Of all the examples of grief in the Bible, there is one that stands head and shoulders above the rest: 2 Samuel 12:18–23.

David is experiencing what no parent expects to face—the death of a child. His newborn son is very sick and will die. For seven days, David fasted, prayed, and laid on the ground all night. When others tried to lift him up and encourage him to eat, he refused. After seven days, the child died. And to the astonishment of those around him, David did the unthinkable. His response is as follows:

1. He Accepted the Irreversible

Upon hearing the news of his son's death, David got up, washed, anointed himself, and changed his clothes. These actions signified that David knew there was nothing more he could do. God responded to his prayer, fasting, and humility with a resounding no! The only alternatives before him were to blame God, blame himself (he would have been right if he did), or accept God's will. He chose the latter.

Death and life are in the hands of the Almighty. Jesus came in order to destroy him who had the power of death, Satan. And Jesus, upon His resurrection, became victorious over death, hell, and the grave (Hebrews 2:14; Revelation 1:18; Matthew 27:53).

When the Lord takes our loved ones in death, it is He and He alone Who has the power to impart life to them again. So when we have prayed earnestly for their recovery and God says no, then we need to accept it as God's perfect will. This is the first step to overcoming grief.

2. He Puts God First

For seven days, David went without food. Surely, he was hungry and eating would have been natural. Instead, David went to the House of God and worshiped Him. Physical food is necessary, but it cannot accomplish what spiritual manna from heaven can.

His choice to worship God before eating demonstrated two important truths. First, he was willing to trust God's decision about the child. Second, he was ready to let go of what he could not change.

If there is ever a time one needs to draw near to God, it is when a loved one dies. All communication, all dependency, all companionship, and all affection have ceased at death.

Yet the Lord has promised, *"When my father and mother forsake me, then the LORD will take me up. My help cometh from the Lord, which made heaven and earth. He will not suffer thy foot to be moved: he that keepeth thee will not slumber"* (Psalm 27:10, 121:3–4).

My friend, leaving God out of the equation and forsaking the assembling of yourself together with God's people at God's house is a grave mistake. Putting God first is essential to overcoming grief.

3. He Doesn't Give Up on Life

The death of a loved one is not the end of life. God had a purpose and plan for David. He has the same for you and me. David returned to the throne and reigned as king for another fifteen to twenty years.

Holding on to the past will hinder one from moving toward the future. The Apostle Paul spoke about *"forgetting those things which are behind, and reaching forth unto those things which are before, I press toward the mark for the prize of the high calling of God in Christ Jesus"* (Philippians 3:13–14).

Paul is not addressing grief directly in this passage. However, he is using his past circumstances as an illustration of a hindrance. Paul as well as all of us had a past. I feel pretty confident that early in his Christian walk with God, Paul's past activities brought him grief.

He had put to death many Christians before his conversion. Paul came to the place that he knew he could not change the past. He had to either commit it completely to God and move on, or stay stuck where he was. He chose to give it over to God, not saying he ever forgot it: nevertheless, his past would not hinder his future in serving the Lord.

No one, especially in the death of a child, will ever get over it and completely forget it. Nevertheless, by the grace of God, an individual can, one step at the time, move forward to the glory of God.

4. He Displays Great Confidence in God

Listen to the words of David: *"But now he is dead, wherefore should I fast? can I bring him back again? I shall go to him, but he shall not return to me"* (2 Samuel 12:23).

There cannot be a more devastating experience than the death of a child. Such a loss brings with it an overwhelming sense of grief and pain. It is a life-altering experience that taxes the whole of the parents as they try to move forward without their child.

J.J. Jasper said, "A radio talk show host lost his son in a go-cart tragedy. He compared the loss of his son to that of an amputation."

Does one ever forget an amputated limb? No. Is life ever the same? No. Are the daily activities a little more difficult? Yes. Can one adjust to the loss and manage without it? Only by the grace of God.

There will be many events that will cause them to relive that horrific day. And the last thing they need on their mind is where is my child, who are they with, and what are they doing? David assures us that children who die before the age of accountability are in heaven.

David also assures the believer concerning his security in Christ. Even though David was a man after God's own heart, he was far from perfect. David had sinned against God, which resulted in the death of his son. But David knew his eternity was secure. Listen to his words: "*I shall go to him, but he shall not return to me.*"

However, before we leave this section on grief, there is one situation I'd like to address. Suppose the loved who died was not a Christian. Then, it is for certain that he or she is not in heaven but in hell.

I know there are a lot of opinions concerning the destiny of the dead. I understand the desire for all to believe our loved ones are in a better place. However, in order to believe there is a better place, one must accept there is a worse place. And if this world is as bad as it gets, then why did Jesus die on the cross? His death would be absolutely ridiculous if this world is the worst it ever gets.

But, and if there is a place worst this world, a place of suffering beyond human comprehension, then the death of Christ makes perfect sense.

The name Jesus was given to Him because it represented the reason why He was born and had died. "Jesus" means Saviour or Deliverer. Upon His birth, Joseph was instructed to call His name Jesus "*for he shall save his people from their sins*" (Matthew 1:21).

Jesus died on the Cross to save or to deliver us from the penalty of sin (Romans 6:23). That penalty is separation from God in a place of eternal torments called hell (Revelation 14:9–11). His payment for our sins is not universally applied to anyone's account (John 1:11–13).

"*He came unto his own, and his own received him not. But as many as received him, to them gave the right to become the sons of God, even to them that believe on his name: Which were born, not of blood, nor of the will of the flesh, nor of the will of man, but of God.*"

This payment or gift of God is received by faith alone (Ephesians 2:8–9). No good works, moral goodness, nor sincere religious activity is acceptable to God (Titus 3:3–7). One must see his or her depravity, acknowledge their sinfulness, believe Jesus died personally for them, and call out to the Lord Jesus for forgiveness and salvation (Romans 10:9–10, 13). When an individual receives Jesus Christ as their personal Saviour, then and only then are they fit for heaven.

If my loved one is in hell, then how do I overcome the grief knowing he or she is suffering for eternity? The answer is not profound, nor is it degrading. You overcome your grief by the truths of the Word of God.

Whether you who are reading these words are a Christian or not, there are amazing revelations in the Bible that can put your grief to rest.

The first is in Luke 16:19–31. God pulls back the curtain and allows us to hear a conversation in hell. The rich, who is in hell, made this request: "*Then he said, I pray thee therefore, father, that thou wouldest send him to my father's house: For I have five brethren; that he may testify unto them, lest they also come into this place of torment.*"

Here's the truth of this passage. If you are not a Christian, those who are in hell do not desire your grief or your tears. They desire and plead that you would receive Jesus Christ as your Saviour and not "*come into this place of torment.*" They would say, "Please stop grieving and get saved!"

However, if I am a Christian and my loved one is in hell, how can I not grieve? The answer is the same for you—the truth of God's Word. We must accept the fact that we can't change their eternal destiny. We can only strive to live a life that's pleasing unto God and witness to as many as we can about the Lord Jesus. While understanding that we may, from time to time, think about their eternal abode, nevertheless, there is comfort found in God's promises. "*And God shall wipe away all tears from their eyes; and there shall be no more death, neither sorrow, nor crying, neither shall there be any more pain: for the former things are passed away. And he that set upon the throne said, Behold, I make all things new*" (Revelation 21:4–5).

There is coming a day when God removes the memory of former things from minds of the saints of God. There will be no more sorrow and grief as promised by God himself. Until then, we rest in the power of God's promises, and we take our burdens to the Lord and leave them there.

Can We Know Where We Will Spend Eternity before We Die?

J. C. Stevens addresses this question: "Many are still convinced that ultimately salvation can only be determined after death when they stand before God's judgment."

Do we really have to wait until death to know for sure? What an awful disappointment it would be to live this life to the best of one's ability only to stand before God and hear Him say, "*I never knew you: depart from me, ye that work iniquity*" (Matthew 7:23).

What Does the Bible Say?

God desires for you *to know* where you will spend eternity, and He has put it in writing. "*These things have I written unto you that believe on the name of the Son of God; that ye may know that ye have eternal life, and that ye may believe on the name of the Son of God*" (1 John 5:13).

God has not made salvation complicated, confusing, or mysterious. That would defeat the whole purpose on John 3:16–17: "*For God so loved the world, that he gave his only begotten Son, that whosoever believeth in him should not perish, but have everlasting life. For God sent not his Son into the world to condemn the world; but that the world through him might be saved.*"

God desires that you know before you die. He wants you to know right now—today. He longs for you to know and enjoy His salvation as a present possession. Listen:

> *He that believeth on him* is *not condemned: but he that believeth not* is *condemned already.* (John 3:18)

> *He that* believeth *on the Son hath everlasting life: and he that believeth not the Son shall not see life; but the wrath of God abideth on him.* (John 3:36)

> *He that heareth my word, and believeth on him that sent me, hath everlasting life, and shall not come into condemnation; but is passed from death unto life.* (John 5:24)

> *He that believeth on me hath everlasting life.* (John 6:47)

> *Whosoever believeth that Jesus is the Christ is born of God.* (1 John 5:1)

> *And this is the record, that God* hath given to us eternal life, *and this life is in his Son. He that* hath *the Son hath life; and he that hath not the Son of God hath not life.* (1 John 5:11–12)

Notice that every one of these verses are written in the present tense. He that hears and believes is not condemned, has everlasting life, is born of God, and God has given him—right now—eternal life. However, for those who don't believe, God says they are condemned *already*, the wrath of God *already abides* on them and they do not have eternal life.

These verses clearly state that you can know right now whether you are saved and on the way to heaven or you are not saved and on the way to hell. If you are in the latter group, you do not have to remain there. Your eternal destiny can be changed instantly by repenting of your sins and asking Jesus to be your Saviour. Therefore, according to the Bible, you can know where you are going before you die.

Is there any evidence or testimony that will corroborate this? Yes. There is the witness of six people who say you can know. Jesus said that only two witnesses were needed to establish the truth; therefore, six is more than sufficient (Deuteronomy 17:6; Matthew 18:16). These witnesses are David (2 Samuel 12:22–23; Psalm 23:1–6), Job (Job 19:25–27), Elijah (2 Kings 2:1–11), the thief on the cross (Luke 23:39–43), Stephen (Acts 7:54–60), and last of all, Paul in 2 Timothy 4:6–8.

May I call your attention to 2 Timothy 4:8: "*Henceforth there is laid up for me a crown of righteousness, which the Lord the righteous judge, shall give me at that day: and not to me only, but unto all them also that love his appearing.*"

H.A. Ironside said, "He is not thinking of himself only. He was not the only one who will have a crown of righteousness. *It is for all them also* that love Christ's appearing" (italics mine). Do you love His appearing? Are you waiting for the coming of the Lord Jesus Christ? Is that the lodestar of your soul? We read, "Every man that hath this hope in him purifieth himself, even as He is pure" (1 John 3:3).

The hope of the coming of the Lord is the most sanctifying thing I know. If you are living day by day as one expecting the early return of your Lord, you are not going to be carried away by the trend of the times and you are not going to yield to the solicitations of the world, the flesh, and the devil.

The fact of Christ's return changes the life of the true believer and assures him or her that heaven awaits them even if they die before He comes.

Four Concerns about the Bible

However, some question the authority of the Bible. Can it be trusted, they ask. After all, *it was written by man,* and we know that man is prone to make mistakes. Therefore, the Bible must contain mistakes.

And then, what about *interpretation?* Two people can read the same passage of scripture and have two completely different opinions as to its meaning. Is one right and the other wrong? Who makes that determination?

Still, others argue *relevance.* The Bible is old and outdated. It might have been all right at the time it was written. But things have changed, man is more highly educated, and the truth is what you perceive it to be.

Finally, there is the *traditionalist.* They will only accept biblical teachings which agree with those things passed down to them by their predecessors. Their normal response is, "This is what I have been taught all my life."

I understand these concerns about the Bible. I also understand that unless one is convinced that the Bible is the Word of God and the final authority in all spiritual matters, one will never have peace about their eternal destiny.

It is true man wrote the Bible. However, he is not the author or originator of the Bible. In 2 Peter 1:21 we read, "*For the prophecy came not in old time by the will of man: but holy men of God spake as they were moved by the Holy Ghost.*" Time will not allow for an in-depth study of this verse. Nevertheless, three truths are set forth in this verse.

First, the Bible is not man's idea. "*For the prophecy came not… by the will of man*" (2 Peter 1:21). Second, God did not just use any man; He used "*holy men of God.*" Third, what these men wrote were not their own words but that which the Holy Spirit inspired them to write: "*Spake as they were moved by the Holy Ghost.*"

Allow me to use a courtroom stenographer to illustrate what this verse is saying. A stenographer records every word spoken during a trial. When he or she is called upon to read what an individual has testified, whose words are being read? If you agree that he or she is reading the words of the witness, then in like manner, when you read the Bible, you are not reading the words and thoughts of the human writers but the very words and thoughts of God.

All these concerns—man, interpretation, relevance, and tradition—are just tools Satan uses to hinder people from knowing the truth. Second Peter 1:20 addresses the matter of interpretation: *"Knowing this first, that no scripture is of any private interpretation."* This means that no individual verse or passage of scripture stands alone. It is not subject to its own interpretation, nor by theologians, preachers, or any individual. The only way to understand what a verse or passage really means is by comparing scripture with scripture (1 Corinthians 2:14). Private interpretation leads to misinterpretation.

As for relevance, the Bible is more up-to-date than the local newspaper or the news broadcast. All one has to do is read passages like Genesis 6:5; 1 Timothy 4:1–3; 2 Timothy 3:1–7; 2 Timothy 4:1–4 and other passages like Matthew 24:1–14 to understand the relevance of the Bible. It not only reveals society as we know it today, but it shows how the things of today are setting the stage for the future judgment of God.

And for the traditionalist, Jesus addressed that in Matthew 5. Six times Jesus compared what His audience had heard and what the truth really is. Read Matthew 5:21–22, 27–28, 31–34, 38–39, and 43–44. Jesus says each time, *"Ye have heard… but I say unto you."* When tradition and the Bible collide, it is always wise to side with the Bible. Many a person did not and would not go to heaven because of tradition. They attend this particular church and base their beliefs solely on what their parents, grandparents, and their grand-grand-parents said. My friend, tradition is dangerous unless it agrees with the Word of God.

There are over nine hundred references in the Old Testament that claim the Bible is the Word of God. The Apostle Paul assured us what he wrote was not his own words: *"But I certify you, brethren, that the gospel which was preached of me is not after man. For I neither received it of man, neither was I taught it, but by the revelation of Jesus Christ"* (Galatians 1:11–12). He also affirms the totality of the Bible being God's Word from Genesis to Revelation: *"All scripture is given by inspiration of God"* (2Timothy 3:16).

The Lord Himself never expressed His own words but the Father's. *"For I have not spoken of myself; but the Father which sent me, he gave me a commandment, what I should say, and what I should speak. And I know that his commandment is life everlasting: whatsoever I speak therefore, even as the Father said unto me, so I speak"* (John 12:49–50).

If the Bible is not God's Word, then anyone's opinion is just as good as the other. However, it is God's Word; therefore, opinions do not matter. God said it and that settles it. God says you can know: *"These things have I written unto you that believe on the name of the Son of God; that ye may know that ye have eternal life, and that ye may believe on the name of the Son of God"* (1 John 5:13). Whom will you believe: God or man? *"Let God be true and but every man a liar... If we receive the witness of men, the witness of God is greater"* (Romans 3:4; 1 John 5:9).

Two Misunderstandings

I believe there are two reasons why many people say you just can't know until after death.

1. The Misunderstanding of Salvation

The average person, whether religious or nonreligious, equate going to heaven with good deeds or works. Therefore, if my good works outweigh my bad works, God will allow entrance into His kingdom. However, this perception of salvation is foreign to the Bible.

Here are just a few of the passages which refute the idea of salvation by works: Romans 4:1–4, 5:1, 11:6; 1 Corinthians 1:29–31; 2 Timothy 1:9; Titus 3:4–7; and Ephesians 2:8–9. I would like to focus your attention on the Ephesians passage. *"For by grace are ye saved through faith; and that not of yourselves: it is the gift of God: Not of works, lest any man should boast"* (Ephesians 2:8–9).

This verse eliminates three things:

- Yourselves. Salvation does not find its origin in us. All that you and I have to offer or contribute toward our salvation is *sin*.
- Works. We can't earn God's salvation. If we could, how many would it take? And since God doesn't say, then you will never know if you'll have enough when you die!
- Boasting. If salvation were obtained by our efforts, that would give us bragging rights, and this verse eliminates that.

This verse emphasizes three things:

- Grace, God's unmerited favor. Earlier, we addressed the thief on the cross and deathbed repentance. Now if going to heaven were based on good deeds, what good deed did the thief have to offer God? He definitely had not kept the law given by Moses. He was never baptized. He never gave a dime to charity, and most assuredly, he did not love his neighbor as himself. All he had was his sin! He had nothing else to offer God.

  He was absolutely guilty of breaking God's law, bankrupt of any righteousness (good deeds), and doomed to an eternal hell. Nevertheless, God by grace alone, without any good deeds, took that thief to Paradise when he died. "Amazing grace, how sweet the sound that saved a wretch like me" shall be the theme of the heart and lips of this thief throughout eternity. *"Being justified freely by his grace through the redemption that is in Christ Jesus"* (Romans 3:24).
- Faith—trusting, depending, or relying fully on God to do for me what I cannot do myself. There has never been a greater demonstration of faith than when the thief said, "Lord, remember me when thou comest into thy kingdom." This man could no more pay his sin debt to God

than you or I can perform open-heart surgery on ourselves. As we must depend totally on the surgeon to perform the necessary surgery lest we die, we, like the thief on the cross, must fully trust Jesus to pay our sin debt lest we spend eternity in hell. *"But without faith it is impossible to please him; for he that cometh to God must believe that he is, and that he is the rewarder of them that diligently seek him"* (Hebrews 11:6).

- Gift, something that's given to us without price or payment on our part. Salvation is a gift which is offered to all who will receive it by faith from the giver—God.

> *"He came unto his own, and his own received him not. But as many as received him, to them gave he power to become the sons of God, even to them that believe on his name: Which were born, not of blood, nor of the will of the flesh, nor of the will of man, but of God"* (John 1:11–13).

Carefully consider this statement: Salvation is either

- totally and completely of God
- the joint effort of God and man
- totally and completely of man

If it is the latter, totally and completely of man, then man has no need of the Saviour. He is able by his own efforts to lift himself out of the ruins of total depravity and present himself faultless before God. However, God sees mankind from a different point of view. This is how God describes man.

> *But we are all as an unclean thing, and all our righteousnesses are as filthy rags; and we all do fade as a leaf; and our iniquities, like the wind, have taken us away.* (Isaiah 64:6)

> *Verily every man at his best state is altogether*
> *vanity. Selah.* (Psalm 39:5)

> *And the* whole world *lieth in wickedness.*
> (1 John 5:17)

Now if it is the middle, a joint effort of God and man, then failure on the part of either would terminate the contract of salvation. Now if God fails to do His part, then He has lied, is untrustworthy, and powerless to keep me out of hell. Therefore I perish because God failed to do His part. However, if I fail to do my part, then God is not obligated to keep His part and the results would be the same—no salvation.

John MacArthur said, "If any part of my eternal salvation depends upon my power, ability, commitment or righteousness, I won't get there."

Charles Spurgeon said, "No man can keep himself, he'll surely fall. If left to ourselves, we'll go to hell. Only Jesus can save us from our sins." And my friend, only Jesus can keep us saved! To think otherwise reveals a misunderstanding concerning the total depravity of the human nature.

There is no joint effort between God and me in this matter of salvation. If it were, then I would be able to share in God's glory, but not according to God: "*I am the Lord: that is My name: and My glory will I not give to another, neither My praise to graven images… I will not give My glory unto another*" (Isaiah 42:8, 48:11).

But if it is the first, and by the way it is totally and completely of God, then it is God Who saves, it is God Who keeps, and it is God Who guarantees our safe arrival to heaven.

> *For this is good and acceptable in the sight of*
> *God our Saviour; Who will have all men to be saved,*
> *and come to the knowledge of the truth… because*
> *we trust in the living God, who is the Saviour of*
> *all men, specially of those that believe.* (1 Timothy
> 2:3,5, 4:10)

For God sent not his Son into the world to condemn the world; but that the world through him might be saved. (John 3:17)

Who are kept by the power of God through faith unto salvation ready to be revealed in the last time. (1 Peter 1:5)

All that the Father giveth me shall come to me; and he that cometh to me I will in no wise cast out... And this is the Father's will which hath sent me, that of all which he hath given me I should lose nothing, but should raise it up again at the last day... and I will raise him up at the last day. (John 6:37, 39, 40)

In my Father's house are many mansions: if it were not so, I would have told you. I go to prepare a place for you. And if I go and prepare a place for you, I will come again, and receive you unto myself; that where I am there ye may be also. (John 14:2–3)

But God who is rich in mercy, for his great love wherewith he loved us, Even when we were dead in sins, hath quickened us together with Christ, (by grace ye are saved;) *And hath raised us up together and made us sit together in heavenly places in Christ Jesus: That in the ages to come he might shew the exceeding riches of his grace in his kindness toward us through Christ Jesus.* (Ephesians 2:4–7)

Now unto him that is able to keep you from falling, and to present you faultless before the presence of his glory with exceeding joy. (Jude 1:24)

Salvation is a gift from God. You can't buy it, earn it, nor afford to be without it. You and I have absolutely nothing to offer God for His gift of salvation. However, it is available to anyone who will admit to God: I am a sinner, I believe that Jesus died for my sins and will ask God to forgive all my sins for Jesus's sake. He will do it if you ask Him too.

> *That if thou shalt confess with thy mouth the Lord Jesus, and shalt believe in thine heart that God hath raised him from the dead, thou shalt be saved. For with the heart man believeth unto righteousness; and with the mouth confession is made unto salvation. For whosoever shall call upon the name of the Lord shall be saved.* (Romans 10:9–10, 13)

> *In hope of eternal life, which God, that cannot lie, promised before the world began.* (Titus 1:2)

2.   Misunderstanding the Resurrection

The biggest misconception concerning the resurrection is the idea of a general resurrection. This idea supposes that everyone will be raised at the same time to stand before God. However, a careful study of the Bible reveals this is not the case.

The assumption of a general resurrection comes when certain passages of scripture are isolated and not taken in light of the Bible as a whole. A couple of examples:

> *And many of them that sleep* [have died] *in the dust of the earth shall awake, some to everlasting life, and some to shame and everlasting contempt.* (Daniel 12:2)

> *Marvel not at this: for the hour is coming, in which all that are in the graves shall hear his voice, And shall come forth; they that have done*

*good, unto the resurrection of life; and they that
have done evil, unto the resurrection of damnation.*
(John 5:28–29)

Lehman Strauss said, "Nowhere in scripture are we taught that
the bodies of all men will be raised at the same time. It is true that
all the dead will be raised and brought into judgment, but neither
the time, the place, nor the judgment are the same. The Bible clearly
distinguishes between a first and second resurrection. When men are
raised, not all will be raised at the same time nor in the same condition. There will be two resurrections for two classes of people. One
will be raised to eternal life… while the other will be raised to eternal
damnation."

Nevertheless, the Bible clearly teaches that these two resurrections are separated by a thousand years.

*And I saw thrones, and they that sat upon
them, and judgement was given unto them: and I
saw the souls of them that were beheaded for the
witness of Jesus, and for the word of God, and which
had not worshipped the beast, neither his image,
neither received his mark upon their foreheads, or in
their hands: and they lived and reigned with Christ
a thousand years.*

*But the rest of the dead lived not again until
the thousand years were finished. This is the first
resurrection. Blessed and holy is he that hath part
in the first resurrection: on which the second death
hath no power, but they shall be priest of God and of
Christ, and shall reign with him a thousand years.
And when the thousand years are expired… And
I saw a great white throne… And I saw the dead
great and small, stand before God… And the sea
gave up the dead… and death and hell delivered up
the dead which were in them: and they were judged*

every man according to their works... This is the second death. (Revelation 20:4–15)

The order of the resurrections is as follows: all who have received Jesus Christ as their Saviour will be in the first resurrection while those who rejected Him will be in the second resurrection a thousand years later.

Those who are saved will be in the first resurrection and will stand before God at the Judgment Seat of Christ to receive their due reward (1 Corinthians 3:11–15; Romans 14:9–10; 2 Corinthians 5:10). Meanwhile, the unsaved will be raised a thousand years later to stand before God at the Great White Throne Judgment where they will be cast into the lake of fire for all eternity (Revelation 20:15).

The truth of the matter is our eternal destiny is determined before the resurrection, not afterward. The resurrection only reveals when and where we'll stand before God. Which resurrection will you be in: the first or the second?

Is It Possible to Know to Some Degree Where Others Are Who Have Died?

I think it was Warren Wiersbe who saw this inscription on a tombstone which caught his attention:

> Pause my friend as you pass by
> As you are so once was I
> As I am so you will be
> Prepare thyself to follow me

As he pondered this saying and the truth it contained, Warren Wiersbe wrote these words:

> To follow you is not my intent
> Till I know which way you went

Previously, I asked you, when have you ever been to a funeral and heard these words: "We are gathered here today to honor the memory and life of _____. He is survived by his wife _____ of _____ years. His has two sons _____ and _____. One daughter _____ and her husband _____ and their twin children _____ and _____. However, I stand before you this day with a broken heart, not for those who have survived, but for _____, because he is in hell today!"

I think the answer is never! I went on to say that the statement would be true in every case where the deceased did not receive the Lord Jesus Christ as Saviour. However, I said it would not be well received by family and friends. Many would find it distasteful, offensive, and unpleasant. Some would accuse the speaker of being insensitive and judgmental while others would opt for "deathbed repentance" saying he or she could have asked God for forgiveness before death.

I agree with the truth of those statements; however, I would encourage you to remember the words of Matthew Henry: "It is certain that true repentance is never too late, but it is as certain that late repentance is seldom true… Be sure that in general men die as they live."

So is it possible to know to some degree where others are who have died? The short answer is yes; however, it is important to understand that only God is omniscient. He alone knows each heart. Nevertheless, God has provided a way by which each individual reveals what is in their own heart. All we need to do is observe one's actions in order to know what's in their heart. This old saying sums it up: Actions speak louder than words. What is seen outwardly is first found inwardly.

Beware of false prophets, which come to you in sheep's clothing, but inwardly they are ravening wolves. Ye shall know them by their fruits. Every tree that bringeth not forth good fruit is hewn down and cast into the fire. Wherefore by their fruits ye shall know them. (Matthew 7:15–16, 19:20).

But those things which proceed out of the mouth come from the heart; and they defile the man. For out of the heart proceed evil thoughts, murders, adulteries, fornications, thefts, false wit-

ness, blasphemies: These are the things which defile a man. (Matthew 15:18–20).

He that committeth sin is of the devil; for the devil sinneth from the beginning. In this the children of God are manifest, and the children of the devil: whosoever doeth not righteousness is not of God, neither he that loveth not his brother. (1 John 3:8, 10).

For as he thinketh in his heart, so is he. (Proverbs 23:7)

The character and lifestyle of an individual is the method God has given us to know the heart of another. What's in the heart determines the character, and that character is reflected in one's lifestyle.

Curtis Hudson said, "We are not sinners because we sin. We sin because we are sinners." In other words, a person is not a thief because he steals. He steals because he is a thief at heart. Again, a man is not a liar because he lies. He lies because he is a liar at heart. Once more, a man is not a murderer because he kills. He kills because he is a murderer at heart.

Consider carefully the following passages of scripture. In them, God describes the actions or lifestyle of those who will not be in heaven.

Know ye not that the unrighteous shall not inherit the kingdom of God? Be not deceived: neither fornicators, nor idolaters, nor adulterers, nor effeminate, nor abusers of themselves with mankind, Nor thieves, nor covetous, nor drunkards, nor revilers, nor extortioners, shall inherit the kingdom of God. (1 Corinthians 6:9–10)

Now the works of the flesh are manifest, which are these; Adultery, fornication, uncleanness, lasciviousness, Idolatry, witchcraft, hatred, variance, emu-

lations, wrath, strife, seditions, heresies, Envyings, murders, drunkenness, revellings, and such like: of the which I tell you before, as I have also told you in time past, that they which do such things shall not inherit the kingdom of God. (Galatians 5:19–21)

But fornication, and all uncleanness, or covetousness, let it not be once named among you, as becometh saints; Neither filthiness, nor foolish talking, nor jesting, which are not convenient: but rather giving of thanks. For this ye know, that no whoremonger, nor unclean person, nor covetous man, who is an idolater, hath any inheritance in the kingdom of Christ and of God. Let no man deceive you with vain words: for because of these things cometh the wrath of God upon the children of disobedience. (Ephesians 5:3–6)

But the fearful, and unbelieving, and the abominable, and murderers, and whoremongers, and sorcerers, and idolaters, and all liars, shall have their part in the lake which burneth with fire and brimstone: which is the second death. (Revelation 21:8)

These are some of the most sobering words in the entire Bible. Why? No matter how bad we desire for our loved ones or friends to be in heaven, on the authority of God himself, those whom He describes in these verses will not be there! It doesn't matter how good the individual may have been. They could be the kind of person who would have given you the shirt off their back, the last dime in their pocket, or have gone a hundred miles out of the way to meet someone's need, yet God said it and that settles it. They will not *inherit the kingdom of God but shall have their part in the lake of fire which burneth with fire and brimstone.*

It is not easy to accept that a loved one or friend is in hell. However, denying the scriptures before us and the authority of God will not change nor end their eternity of suffering. The only comfort, if it could be considered comfort, in facing the reality of their eternal damnation is that your loved one or friend does not desire your presence in such an awful place (Luke 16:27–31).

I can't close this chapter without addressing one more thing. Death will produce the greatest surprise of all time. When an individual dies and reaches their eternal abode, they will be surprised as to who is and is not there. There will be people in hell who will be surprised at the preachers, deacons, Sunday school teachers, and the religious crowd who will occupy a place there. There will be those in heaven who will be surprised at the drunks, drug dealers, prostitutes, murderers, and so on who will occupy a mansion beside them.

It is true that God alone knows the heart. However, it is also true that the religious crowd is the hardest for us to evaluate. This group talks the talk and seemingly walks the walk, yet God says they are not His. Why? Misplaced faith!

These are sincere and devout people: they attend church regularly, give to charity, teach, sing in the choir, serve on numerous committees, help their neighbors, and do many wonderful things in the name of God. Nevertheless, they won't be in heaven because they are trusting in their deeds and not in Christ. Read carefully.

> *And he spake this parable unto certain which trusted in themselves that they were righteous, and despised others: Two men went up into the temple to pray; the one a Pharisee, and the other a publican.*
>
> *The Pharisee stood and prayed thus with himself, God, I thank thee, that I am not as other men are, extortioners, unjust, adulterers, or even as this publican. I fast twice in the week, I give tithes of all that I possess.*
>
> *And the publican, standing afar off, would not lift up so much as his eyes unto heaven, but smote upon his breast, saying, God be merciful to me a sinner. I tell you, this man went down to his house justified rather than the other: for every one*

that exalteth himself shall be abased; and he that humbleth himself shall be exalted. (Luke 18:9–14)

Not every one that saith unto me, Lord, Lord, shall enter into the kingdom of heaven; but he that doeth the will of my Father which is in heaven. Many will say to me in that day, Lord, Lord, have we not prophesied in thy name? and in thy name have cast out devils? and in thy name done many wonderful works? And then will I profess unto them, I never knew you: depart from me, ye that work iniquity. (Matthew 7:21–23)

Where is your faith today? If I could personally speak to you in private, if I were someone with whom you were comfortable talking about religious matters, and if I could ask you these two questions, what would your answers be?

Where will you spend eternity when you die? If your answer is heaven, the second and most important question would be why would you go to heaven when you die?

Before you answer, let me share a true story with you. I had gained the trust of a man and his wife. They had become comfortable talking to me about spiritual matters. One afternoon while visiting, the wife looked at me and asked this question: Where do you think I'll go when I die?

I responded with this: Let me ask you two questions first. Where do you think you will go when you die? Her response was *heaven!* I responded with the second question. Why?

I knew, because of the friendship that had developed between us, that the answer she was about to give would reveal where she had placed her faith. Her answer was, "Because I have been baptized."

My response: According to your answer, you will split hell wide open. I proceeded with several more questions to which there were no responses. Those questions were: If baptism could wash away your sin, why was Jesus baptized? He had no sin. If baptism could wash away your sin, what about the thief on the cross? He wasn't baptized.

If the Old Testament people were saved by keeping the law, how did they get saved before the law was given? And finally, if baptism could wash away your sins, then why did God allow His only Son to die such an excruciating death?

You could have heard a pin drop a thousand miles away. I left an angry lady that day. She did not like my answer, nor will many of those who may be reading these words. Nevertheless, I told her the truth.

But that's not the end of the story! A few weeks later, she and her husband came to a revival meeting. On Friday night of that meeting, both came forward in the invitation and put their faith and trust in Jesus Christ as their Saviour alone. From that night to the day she died, she said, "Preacher, now I'm not afraid to die."

My friend, you and I have talked a lot about spiritual matters as you have read this book. Would you be comfortable with me asking you a couple of questions? Are you afraid to die? Are you sure you would go to heaven when you die? Where have you placed your faith: in Jesus alone or in your good works? God has said, "*For by grace are ye saved through faith; and that not of yourselves: it is the gift of God: Not of works, lest any man should boast*" (Ephesians 2:8–9).

If you want to go to heaven when you die, you'll have to go God's way. It is His heaven, just as your home is yours. He has the right to say who is and who is not entering, just as you do at your home. His has the right to set the requirements for entrance into His presence, just as you do when someone knocks at your door. It's God's heaven; do you want to go? Are you willing to go His way? His way is not difficult. His requirements are:

- First, realize you are a sinner. "*For* all *have sinned and come short of the glory of God*" (Romans 3:23).
- Second, understand you are not good enough to go as you are. "*There is none righteousness, no, not one… there is none that doeth good, no, not one… all our righteousnesses are as filthy rags*" (Romans 3:10, 12; Isaiah 64:6).
- Third, remember God will not accept your good works. "*Not by works of righteousness which we have done, but*

according to his mercy he saved us… not of works, lest any should boast" (Titus 3:5; Ephesians 2:9).

- Fourth, believe that Jesus died for your sins. *"For I deliver unto you first of all… how that Christ died for our sins according to the scriptures; And that he was buried, and rose again the third day according to the scriptures… Surely he hath borne our griefs, and carried our sorrows… But he was wounded for our transgressions, he was bruised for our iniquities: the chastisement of our peace was upon him; and with his stripes we are healed… Who his own self bare our sins in his own body on the tree… For Christ also hath once suffered for our sins, the just for the unjust, that he might bring us to God, being put to death in the flesh but quickened in the Spirit"* (1 Corinthians 15:3–4; Isaiah 53:4–5; 1 Peter 2:24, 3:18).
- Fifth, by faith, receive Jesus Christ as your personal Saviour. What is faith? Biblical faith is simply "believing" God. It is acting on what God has promised in His Word. God has promised, *"For whosoever shall call upon the name of the Lord shall be saved"* (Romans 10:13).

Will you confess to God you are a sinner, that you believe Jesus died for your sins, ask Him to forgive your sins and be your Saviour. If you will, He has promised to save you and allow you to go to heaven when you die. How will you know that for sure?

"In hope of eternal life, which God, that cannot lie, promised before the world began" (Titus 1:2). All things are possible with God, but there is one thing that is impossible for God to do—lie. Call out to God today; He will hear, He will save, and you will be eternally grateful!

Conclusion: Jesus said, *"And ye shall know the truth, and the truth shall make you free"* (John 8:32). God has presented the truth about death and the afterlife in His Word. This truth, if accepted, will give you the confidence you need to face death and eternity. *"For I know whom I have believed, and am persuaded that he is able to keep that which I have committed unto him against that day"* (2 Timothy 1:12).

Send any questions or comments to messengerknox@yahoo.com.

About the Author

Douglas Knox and his wife, Wanda, live in Williamston, North Carolina. They were both born and raised within a few miles of their residence and have called North Carolina home for over sixty years. Wanda is retired, and Douglas is the pastor of Liberty Baptist Church (LBC) in Williamston. He surrendered to the ministry in 1997 and has been the pastor of the LBC for eighteen years. They have two children: Billy (his wife, Robyn) and Allison (her husband, Doug) who have given them five wonderful grandchildren.